# The Power of I AM

## I AM

## Volume 2

Compiled & Edited

By

David Allen

Books for Enlightening and Illuminating the Mind

First Printing, August 2015

ISBN: 978-0-9909643-8-4

Published
by
Shanon Allen
Copyright © 2015

# Introduction

What goes along with the saying of God's name, I AM?

Very little seems to be known, even in today's world, about the mystical nature and power that goes with saying I AM.

The Power of I AM and The Power of I AM Volume 2 will reveal to the reader what the ancients appear to have known about this mystical name.

All day long, mankind is using the name of God and for the most part they are unaware that they are asking for anything, by what they attach to it.

When speaking the name of God . . I AM . . it should be remembered that we should only attach those things that we desire to have happen to us or have in our lives, as our words do not return to us void. Always speak it upward and never downward.

What we attach to our I AM, we are asking for in God's name. To know this, is power.

David Allen

The beginning of each quote is in **bold** print.

# Table of Contents

The ancients knew
that the secret name of God
had power.

Now we do.

**You are told it happened on the Sabbath.** The Sabbath is
only the mystical sense of stillness, when you are
unconcerned, when you are not anxious, when you are not
looking for results, knowing that signs follow and do not
precede. The Sabbath is the day of stillness wherein there is
no working. When you are not working to make it so you are
in the Sabbath. When you are not at all concerned about the
opinion of others, when you walk as though you were, you
cannot raise one finger to make it so, you are in the Sabbath.
I cannot be concerned as to how it will be, and still say I AM
conscious of being it. If I AM conscious of being free, secure,
healthy, and happy, I sustain these states of consciousness
without effort or labor on my part. Therefore, I AM in the
Sabbath.

**God is immovable, unlimited, unchangeable**. The "I AM"
within you never changes, it is always the same, but the
external form changes because it is relative. Yet the
Substance which; is the basis of the form is a Perfect
Substance. Relative things are not realities. Therefore I want
you to recognize that Reality exists everywhere, and is the
basis and the essence of everything. If the external form
seems to you imperfect, the Substance and basis of it all is
perfect. You have heard of miracles, yet they are nothing
more than the perfect action of a Perfect Law that exists
eternally and is omnipresent: present everywhere always.

**The masterful individuality which speaks from the soul is the Supreme Self,** or I AM of God. This I AM is always conscious of Itself. It responds to the man outside as he responds to It. Spirit knows man only at the level of his ability to know himself. Through the spirit . . I AM, we can in the Silence establish a means of communion between the man outside and the Man Inside. Each one of us must contact God through his own mind until He takes possession of our consciousness. The secret of spiritual power is the individual consciousness of union with God. The I AM is Good. It is Love, Life, Law Intelligence and Power, but it interprets Itself to man only as he mentally embodies the whole, only as he recognizes the I AM as the changeless Principle of his own mind. The more completely he becomes conscious of this union, the more power and dominion he expresses. Health, harmony, happiness and prosperity are effects, not causes.

**The name Eve means "elemental life,"** "life," "living." Eve represents the soul region of man and is the mother principle of God in expression through which life is evolved. The I AM (wisdom) puts feeling into what it thinks, and so Eve (feeling) becomes the "mother of all living." Back of feeling is the pure life essence of God. Adam and Eve symbolize the I AM individualized in life and substance. They are the primal elemental forces of Being itself.

**So we see, you must separate the things external to yourselves.** Separate your body, your mind from your real self, YOU. That which you are analyzing cannot be you, can it? It is proof of the fact that it has no power of its own, is it not? Do you not see, the Consciousness is always analyzing something external to itself, but it can never analyze itself. It can never know what It is, but only know that It is. So, do not waste your time trying to find out what it is, only know THAT IT IS, and this is the secret. The more you know that It is, the more will it grow in strength and power. Then you will know "I AM." Immediately you analyze anything external to yourself, even all the forces of the Universe and all in the Universe, even the elements that make up the Universe, you will know they have no power of their own except the power that you give them. You are Spirit individualized. The Eternal Spirit of God is in you, the actual you. Then you will find power and majesty in your Oneness with God. The Consciousness must analyze everything external to itself. When you say "I AM." realize that it is real. The "I AM" enables you to move, think, act and you are using your instruments as a means of expression. The Substance of the Great "I AM" is the Perfect Substance out of which all things are made, the Substance of the Great "I AM," the Substance of God. The Great "I AM" is individualized in you and that enables you to say "I AM." Out of that Substance and in that Substance all things are created and that Substance is perfect in itself. How can any form created in it and out of it have any flaw in it except the individual give it power, who does not understand the Truth?

**Jesus found God to be His (I AM) awareness of being** and so told man that the Kingdom of God and Heaven were within. When it is recorded that Jesus left the world and went to His Father, it is simply stating that He turned His attention from the world of the senses and rose in (I AM) consciousness to that level which He desired to express. There He remained until He became one with the consciousness to which He ascended. When He returned to the world of man, He could act with the positive assurance of that which He was conscious of being, a state of consciousness no one but Himself felt or knew that He possessed. Man who is ignorant of this everlasting law of expression looks upon such happenings as miracles. To rise in consciousness to the level of the thing desired and to remain there until such level becomes your nature is the way of all seeming miracles.

**When he, the Spirit of truth, has come,** he will guide you into all truth. The Spirit of Truth is the I AM of the Universal Mind. When man recognizes that his consciousness is One with the I AM Consciousness, the recognition will guide him into all Truth. We cannot change the truth, but we can change the manifestation of the Law. There is no lack of substance in the great Universal Mind of God, but it is impersonal. Man can always enter the stream of this Universal Substance through the Intelligence and Power of his own I AM, but he can never approach it through the personality or human intellect. Only by surrendering the finite belief in a personal mind and personal self and personal desire that continually tries to demonstrate substance, is it possible to enter the very Substance Itself.

**For your five senses act like five husbands** who constantly
impregnate your consciousness, your I AM, which is the
great womb of GOD; and morning, noon, and night they
suggest to you, and dictate to you that which you must
accept as true. He tells you the one you would like to have
for your husband is not your husband. In other words the
sixth has not yet impregnated you. What you would like to be
is denied by these five, and they hold the power, they dictate
what you will accept as true. What you would like to accept
has not yet penetrated your mind and impregnated your
mind with its reality. He whom you call husband is really not
your husband. You are not bearing his likeness. To bear his
likeness is proof that you are his wife, at least you have
known him intimately. You are not bearing the likeness of
the sixth; you are only bearing the likeness of the five. Then
one turns to me and tells me all that I have ever known. I go
back in my mind's eye and reason tells me that all through
my life I have always accepted the limitations of my senses, I
have always looked upon them as fact; and morning, noon,
and night I have born witness to this acceptance. Reason
tells me I have only known these five from the time I was
born. Now I would like to step outside the limitation of my
senses but I have not yet found within myself the courage to
assume I AM what these five would deny that I AM. So here I
remain, conscious of my task, but without the courage to
step beyond the limitations of my senses, and that which my
reason denies.

**It is on the soul or substance side of consciousness** that ideas are "identified," that is, "named." Whatever we recognize a thing to be, that it becomes to us because of the naming power vested in man (wisdom). "Every beast of the field" and the "cattle" represent ideas of strength, power, vitality, and life. These ideas must be recognized by the I AM before they can be formed. "The birds of the heavens" represent free thoughts and the interchange between the subconscious and the conscious activities of mind. Man has power to name all ideas that are presented to his conscious mind, whether they come from within or without.

**As you progress along the path be not hindered** by words, actions, thoughts or deeds of others. Realize that the Perfect is . . I AM That I AM . . and cannot be made more perfect; but the outer you should respond to the inner. "Be ye perfect as your Father in Heaven is perfect." The "I AM" within each is the Christ of God manifesting in humanity, and when this is realized fully by all, the Fatherhood of God and the Brotherhood of Man will be established upon earth. Then, and then only, will we have supreme happiness. This rests with man, not with God. God has already established this for man, and man has only to accept it by acting according to the Law of God. These words and sayings will affect each and every one of you according to your enlightenment. The "I AM" within is your teacher, and will present to your personal consciousness the message for the moment.

**The Universal Mind is the Self-Conscious,** Self-Knowing, purposeful activity of Spirit. It is at work everywhere and in everything. Even the lowest forms of life reveal the Omnipresent Mind at work. The moneron, the lowest form of independent life, is a perfect model in miniature of our modern submarine. As it inflates and deflates its body in order to rise and sink in the water, it betrays a wonderful intelligence. The spider and the bee show engineering skill that is amazing. The dahlia knows that it must store up starch for the winter while it is growing in the summer. Mind is at work everywhere. It becomes the Consciousness of whatever it contacts. The tree, flower and blade of grass are alive with the Consciousness and Substance of the Universal Mind of God. It is the color, perfume, life and beauty of everything that is. It is the medium through which man comes ultimately to know the truth. Spiritual energy comes from within. The I AM is the source of Divine Energy. It flows through the consciousness of man as an impersonal, silent and Omnipresent Power. Through his soul (subjective mind), man makes his conscious approach to the Universal Mind. To be conscious of It is to be in vital touch with It, to give It conscious direction in body and affairs. Mind meets us at the level of our own understanding and manifests according to our consciousness. Since It cannot give us more than we can receive, we must be consciously receptive to It. Our work in the Silence is dynamic, the results differing according to our various states of consciousness.

**"I AM the Lord, and there is none else,** there is no God beside me." Read these words carefully. They are not my words, they are the inspired words of men who discovered that consciousness is the only reality. If I AM hurt, I AM self hurt. If there is darkness in my world, I created the darkness and the gloom and the depression. If there is light and joy, I created the light and the joy. There is no one but this I AMness that does all. You cannot find a cause outside of your own consciousness. Your world is a grand mirror constantly telling you who you are. As you meet people, they tell you by their behavior who you are. Your prayers will not be less devout because you turn to your own consciousness for help. I do not think that any person in prayer feels more of the joy, the piety, and the feeling of adoration, than I do when I feel thankful, as I assume the feeling of my wish fulfilled, knowing at the same time it is to myself that I turned. In prayer you are called upon to believe that you possess what your reason and your senses deny. When you pray believe that you have and you shall receive.

**I AM the Father of the Living, not the Dead.**" Jesus made this so plain to His disciples; and it is the same today as it was yesterday, and will be the same tomorrow. As the evolutionary process of the great human family progresses, so the various senses that are at present dormant will come to life. When this body is more spiritualized the "I AM," which is the Consciousness in the Substance, will bring them forth, for they are already there. Spirit is all. Then you will see the so-called dead.

**It is to consciousness (I AM) that we must turn** as to the only reality. For there is no clear conception of the origin of phenomena except that consciousness is all and all is consciousness. You need no helper to bring you what you seek. Do not for one second believe that I am advocating escape from reality when I ask you to simply assume you are now the man or the lady that you want to be. If you and I could feel what it would be like were we now that which we want to be, and live in this mental atmosphere as though it were real, then, in a way we do not know, our assumption would harden into fact. This is all we need do in order to ascend to the level where our assumption is already an objective, concrete reality.

## GIVE US THIS DAY OUR DAILY BREAD

**The bread spoken of here** refers not alone to food, clothing and money, but to the Bread of Life. Man shall not live by bread alone, but by every word that proceedeth out of the mouth of God. The law of increase is in the word. I AM is the active agent of creation. It externalizes itself in the substance that coexists with it. I AM the bread of life. Give us this day our daily bread. These words literally mean to you, "I AM positive to the Substance of the I AM here and now. I AM receptive to It. My needs are met." The word give is a command to Substance. You are not begging, pleading or beseeching. You are affirming the Truth, identifying yourself with It and accepting It.

**We must not bring forth untrue expressions.** This is what the majority of people are doing every day by their thoughts, words and actions . . even a word that is unkind is an untrue expression. Do you know what a word really means? Do you know that sound has color and form; that every form has a color and sound; that every audible sound has an invisible color, every visible color an inaudible sound? Even our thoughts have form, color and sound. You have formed the outer expression, but the inner also exists. Realize what your thoughts, words and actions mean. When you understand the power of expression and know the Truth, your knowledge adds power to your word and thought. The "I AM" creates in the invisible world by the voice and by the thoughts; even in the silence we create sound, form and color.

**Now it is absolutely impossible** for you to make this power do anything. You cannot by sheer force of will bend this power to suit your needs. You are not greater than God. You cannot either stop or start this power in its creating, for it is greater than you are and it moves according to law. You cannot say, "I AM going to make money" with all the determination and ferociousness you can muster and expect that you are creating in your experience anything other than belligerence and opposition. You've got to accept, not demand. You can't will anything. This does not mean a doctrine of resignation, far from it. It simply means that you recognize that it is not you who does the creating; it is a power greater than you are. This power creates what you believe and manifests to you what you are prepared to accept. I AM That power.

**Where the consciousness, your I AM, is placed,** you do not have to take the physical body; it gravitates there in spite of you. Things happen to compel you to move in the direction where you are consciously dwelling.

"In my Father's house are many mansions: if it were not so, I would have told you. I go to prepare a place for you. And if I go and prepare a place for you, I will come again, and receive you unto myself; that where I AM, there ye may be also."

The many mansions are the unnumbered states within your mind, for you are the house of God. In my Father's house are unnumbered concepts of self. You could not in eternity exhaust what you are capable of being. If I sit quietly here and assume that I AM elsewhere, I have gone and prepared a place. But if I open my eyes, the bilocation which I created vanishes and I AM back here in the physical form that I left behind me as I went to prepare a place. But I prepared the place nevertheless and will in time dwell there physically. You do not have to concern yourself with the ways and the means that will be employed to move you across space into that place where you have gone and mentally prepared it. Simply sit quietly, no matter where you are, and mentally actualize it.

**No matter what concepts you hold of yourself** it is a limitation. The Truth is not a concept. Dissolve away all limitations, dissolve away all crystallized concepts of Reality and let yourself be I AM That I AM.

**Behold, I AM He that should come...** And the government shall be upon his shoulders. The Presence that will finally rule our lives is now offering a full salvation through our consciousness; but flesh and blood cannot inherit the kingdom. Whilst we are at home in the body (material thought), we are absent from the Lord. All flesh must be spiritualized. We must surrender all ideas of bondage. Our senses are really God's senses; when we realize this, we cannot have poor eyesight, poor hearing, poor health or poor anything. I AM sees through our eyes, hears through our ears, thinks through our minds, works through our bodies. He is All-in-All. I AM declares health and power in every corpuscle, every vein, every cell, every nerve and every atom of the body saying unto them, Be ye therefore perfect even as your Father in heaven is perfect. I AM will fill the body to overflowing with Divine power and Health, for I AM is within every cell, and every cell is alive with the Universal Substance of I AM.

**Like the writer who authors a story,** each of us authors his own life by his choice of what thoughts he will accept and which he will reject. Each of our lives is a story, unfolded by the silent contemplative author who dwells within us, who does nothing more than accept and reject, who is involved only in making choices. This indwelling Self says, "This is so," "This is not so," "I believe this," I feel fine in this circumstance," "I feel badly in this circumstance," "I AM great," "I AM nothing," "There is hope," "There is despair." And each of these choices is manifested in the physical world.

**When you claim that what is true of God** is true of you, miracles will happen in your life. By realizing and knowing these qualities and attributes of God are being expressed through you, and that you are a channel for the Divine, every atom of your being begins to dance to the rhythm of the Eternal God. Beauty, order, harmony, and peace appear in your mind, body, and business world as you feed among the lilies; you feel your oneness with God, Life, and God's Infinite Riches. You are married to your Beloved, for you are now married to God; you are a bride of the Lord (I AM). From this moment forward you will bring forth children of your Beloved; they will bear the image and likeness of their Father and Mother. The father is God's idea; the mother is the emotionalizing of the idea, and its subjective embodiment. From that union of idea and feeling come forth your health, abundance, happiness, and inner peace.

**"Ye shall know the truth and the truth** shall set you free". The truth that sets man free is the knowledge that his (I AM) consciousness is the resurrection and the life, that his consciousness both resurrects and makes alive all that he is conscious of being. Apart from consciousness, there is neither resurrection nor life. When man gives up his belief in a God apart from himself and begins to recognize his awareness of being to be God, as did Jesus and the prophets, he will transform his world with the realization, "I and My Father are one", but "My Father is greater than I".

**The encouraging message in all of this is,** no matter what may be in the subjective state of our thought, the conscious state can change it; this is what treatment does. How can this be done? Through the most direct method imaginable: by consciously knowing that there is no inherited tendency toward limitation, no race suggestion operating through subjectivity, nothing in, around or through us that believes in or accepts limitation in any way, shape, manner or form. We do not stop here, this is only half the treatment. The conscious state must now provide a higher contemplation, a spiritual realization, which says: "I partake of the nature and bounty of the All Good and I AM now surrounded by everything which makes life worthwhile. The Universal Medium at once changes Its thought (because Its thought is deductive only) and says: "Yes, I AM all these things in you," and immediately begins the work of bringing such conditions to pass. Whatever is held in consciousness until it becomes a part of the subjective side of thought, tends to take place in the world of affairs. The reason that we do not demonstrate more easily is that the subjective state of our thought is too often neutralized by the objective state, though often this is an unconscious process of thought.

**"I AM the resurrection and the life."** No principle can carry in itself an opposite and limiting principle contradictory of its own nature, and this is as true of the Principle of Life as of any other principle. It is we who by our thought introduce an opposite and limiting principle and so hinder the working of the principle we are seeking to bring into operation; but so far as the Principle of Life itself is concerned there is in it no reason why it should not come into perfect manifestation here and now.

**"For I the Lord thy God am a jealous God".** . . . This means that you must recognize the Living Spirit Almighty (I AM) as supreme and omnipotent and refuse to give power to any created thing. In other words, you should not worship a created thing; you must give all allegiance, loyalty and devotion to the One Presence and Power within you, called I AM, or Spirit. For example, if you are looking for promotion or advancement and you say to yourself: "The boss is blocking my good; but for him I would be promoted and receive greater emoluments," at that moment you have exalted him, a false god. Actually, you are making the boss a god and denying the One Source . . I AM . . from Whom all blessings flow. Your subconscious mind knows that your loyalty is divided and consequently does not respond. You are like the double-minded man, unstable in all your ways. On the one hand he is affirming that I AM is the Source of his supply, meeting all his needs, and then in the next breath he is resenting his employer for not promoting him and increasing his salary. You must never give power to any person, place or thing, for actually you are transferring the power within you to externals. You must give exclusive devotion and loyalty to the One Power within you . . I AM, which responds according to the nature of your thoughts and belief.

**Spirit is the active and Self-Conscious Principle.** Spirit is First Cause or God . . the Absolute Essence of all that is. It is the Great or Universal I AM. Spirit is Conscious Mind and is the Power which knows Itself. It is conscious Being.

**If you are dissatisfied with your present expression** of life, then you must be born again. Rebirth is the dropping of that level with which you are dissatisfied and rising to that level of (I AM) consciousness which you desire to express and possess. You cannot serve two masters or opposing states of consciousness at the same time. Taking your attention from one state and placing it upon the other, you die to the one from which you have taken it and you live and express the one with which you are united. Man cannot see how it would be possible to express that which he desires to be by so simple a law as acquiring the (I AM) consciousness of the thing desired. The reason for this lack of faith on the part of man is that he looks at the desired state through the consciousness of his present limitations. Therefore, he naturally sees it as impossible of accomplishment. One of the first things man must realize is that it is impossible, in dealing with this spiritual law of consciousness, to put new wine into old bottles or new patches on old garments. That is, you cannot take any part of the present consciousness into the new state. For the state sought is complete in itself and needs no patching. Every level of (I AM) consciousness automatically expresses itself. To rise to the level of any state is to automatically become that state in expression. But, in order to rise to the level that you are not now expressing, you must completely drop the consciousness with which you are now identified. Until your present consciousness is dropped, you will not be able to rise to another level. Do not be dismayed. This letting go of your present identity is not as difficult as it might appear to be. The invitation of the scriptures, "To be absent from the body and be present with the Lord", is not given to a select few; it is a sweeping call to all mankind. The body from which you are invited to escape is your present conception of yourself with all of its limitations, while the Lord with whom you are to be present is your . . I AM . . awareness of being.

**Also realize that in very truth what you see in the mirror**
is but a reflection . . an appearance . . of what your mind
thinks is You. But the Real You, being Spirit, cannot be seen,
and instead is that which sees and knows all things. Now
slowly and very positively . . trying as you voice each word to
realize fully the deep meaning and significance of the
command in them . . speak to that intelligence which you see
looking out of the eyes in the mirror as follows (you can say it
aloud or silently to yourself . . whichever is the most
effective to you): "Be still and know, . . I AM . . God. Know
that I AM, and that you are not at all . . as a separate being. I
AM not your body, mind or soul, . . I AM Spirit. I AM That
which animates you, which lives you, which is your
intelligence, which is your power to be and to do all that you
are and do. "I AM your REAL self . . your ONLY self . . I, the
God of you. You are only a portion of My Consciousness,
dwelling within a focalized center of My Mind, which you call
yourself. The proof is, you are nothing, know nothing, can do
nothing, only as I inspire and empower you to know and do
it."

**It is the polarization of Spirit from the universal** into the
particular, carrying with it all its inherent powers, just as the
smallest flame has all the qualities of fire. The I AM in the
individual is none other than the I AM in the universal. It is
the same Power working in the smaller sphere of which the
individual is the center. This is the great truth which the
ancients set forth under the figure of the Macrocosm and the
Microcosm, the lesser I AM reproducing the precise image of
the greater, and of which the Bible tells us when it speaks of
man as the image of God.

**The person trying to live up to a principle** did not insist that he was greater than the principle, but instead recognized that the principle was greater than he was. Building a god-like self-image was not complex. For the principle of absolute being realized itself by saying, "I AM." And the principle of absolute power realized itself by saying, "I can." And the principle of absolute freedom realized itself by saying, "I don't have to." Desire was the power that accomplished all things. Not willpower. Want power. Desire opened up the pineal gland and allowed pure energy through. A man who wanted something badly developed the power of ten. And the only reason he didn't want something badly was because his desire had been locked up in prison. The bars of that prison were always named, "I AM not," I can't," and "I have to." If you thought, "I AM not," you couldn't choose a goal. If you thought, "I can't," you didn't try to achieve it. If you thought, "I have to," you only went through the motions. In any case, you were a loser. The simple self-image that brought success, whether building bridges or seeking God was "I AM," "I can," and "I don't have to." These enabled you to "want to." By repeating these three affirmations, you could cure yourself of headaches, tiredness, indigestion, irritability, and insomnia. If you fell asleep at night repeating them to yourself, you could get things done that you never thought possible. Only eight little words, but they made a world of difference.

**In the Infinite Consciousness of God** is held the Perfect Image, therefore the Perfect Image is always in existence. The "I AM" in you is the point through which you contact this Divine Consciousness, and this Consciousness becomes, as it were, apparently an individual consciousness to each and every one, but it is not a separate consciousness. When you think separation, and have accepted it, then you have separated yourself mentally from the one great Infinite Consciousness, but it is a false conception. The great Master said: "I and the Father are One." He not only said it, He knew it; it was not a platitude; to Him it was an actual reality. When you recognize this mighty truth, the realization of it gives you control, and everything obeys you. The elements respond to your call, and form according to the image held with this understanding. When this state of consciousness is held, the idea or image held in the consciousness is produced by the Intelligence, and the work is done without effort, the Intelligence always fulfilling the direction of the Consciousness. We make a success of our life when we know this law and apply it with faith. We make a failure of our life when we do not know this law and let in fear and doubt which cause a vacillating action of the Intelligence . . the Mother. But when in Divine meditation with a faithful consciousness, this Mother . . Intelligence . . does the work perfectly and changes the whole nature automatically.

**You are one with the great "I AM" of the universe.** You are part of God. Until you realize that . . and the power it gives you . . you will never know God. "We are parts of one stupendous whole, whose body Nature is, and God the soul." God (I AM) has incarnated Himself in man. He seeks expression. Give Him work to do through you, give Him a chance to express Himself in some useful way, and there is nothing beyond your powers to do or to attain.

It matters not what your age, what your present circumstances or position. If you will seek your help outside your merely physical self, if you will put the God in you into some worthwhile endeavor, and then BELIEVE in Him, you can overcome any poverty, any handicap, any untoward circumstance. Relying upon your personal abilities or riches or friends is being like the heathen of old, whom the Prophet of the Lord taunted. "You have a God whom you must carry," he derided them. "We have a God who carries us!"

The God of personal ability or material riches or friends is one that you must continually carry. Drop him, and immediately you lose everything. But there is a God (I AM) in you who will carry you . . and in the doing of it, provide you with every good thing this world can supply. The purpose of this book is to acquaint you with this God in you, The God That Only The Fortunate Few Know.

As the poet so well expressed it:

"In your own self lies Destiny. Let this
Vast truth cast out all fear, and prejudice,
All hesitation. Know that you are great,
Great with Divinity. So dominate
Environment and enter into bliss.
Love largely and hate nothing. Hold no aim
That does not chord with Universal Good.

Hear what the voices of the Silence say —
All joys are yours if you put forth your claim.
Once let the spiritual laws be understood,
Material things must answer and obey."

Some might think that merely a poet's dream, but along comes Dr. J. B. Rhine of Duke University to prove it scientific fact as well.

In his new book "The Reach of the Mind," Dr. Rhine points out that in the past, Science seemed to feel that man was entirely material. It had discovered how glands regulate personality through their chemical secretions; it had shown that the child mind matures only as the brain develops; that certain mental functions are linked with specific areas of the brain, and that if one of these is injured, the corresponding mental function is lost.

So Science believed that it had accounted for all the processes of thought and action, that it could show a material basis for each.

But now Dr. Rhine and other experimenters have proved that knowledge can be acquired without the use of the senses! Not only that, but they have also proved that the powers of the mind are not bound by space or limited by time! Perhaps their greatest discovery is that the mind can influence matter without physical means.

This has been done through prayer, of course, since time began, but such results have always been looked upon as supernatural. Dr. Rhine and other experimenters show that any normal person has the power to influence objects and events.

To quote "The Reach of the Mind" . . "As a result of thousands of experimental trials, we found it to bc a fact that the mind has a force that can act on matter. . . . There must, therefore, be an energy convertible to physical action, a mental energy."

The one great essential to the successful use of this mental energy seems to be intense interest or desire. The more keyed up a person is, the more eager for results, the more he can influence those results.

Dr. Rhine showed through many experiments that when the subject's interest is distracted, when he lacks ability to concentrate his attention, his mental energy has little or no power over outside objects. It is only as he gives his entire attention to the object in mind, as he concentrates his every energy upon it, that he gets successful results. (Ed. I AM, Meditation and silence are all of benefit here)

Dr. Rhine's experiments prove scientifically what we have always believed . . that there is a Power over and above the merely physical power of the mind or body, that through intense concentration or desire we can link up with that Power, and that once we do, nothing is impossible to us.

It means, in short, that man is not at the mercy of blind chance or Fate, that he can control his own destiny. Science is at last proving what Religion has taught from the beginning . . that God gave man dominion and that he has only to understand and use this dominion to become the Master of his Fate, the Captain of his Soul.

**"Except a man be born again** he cannot enter the kingdom of God."

What is the second birth?

I quietly appropriate that which no man can give me, no woman can give me. I dare to assume that I AM God. This must be of faith, this must be of promise. Then I become the blessed. As I begin to do the things that only this presence could do, I know that I AM born out of the limitations of Ishmael, and I have become heir to the kingdom.

**You may have practiced exercises,** studied philosophies, etc., and no doubt you have gained by them; but when you say I AM That I AM, I AM All there is, my Father and I are one . . you will find that the Divine Intelligence will lead you, it always has and always will. Do not seek for yourself alone, but that others shall also find the way; for he who seeks for himself alone is selfish and limited.

"He who seeks to save his Soul alone
May find the Path but will not reach the Goal;
But he who works in Love may wander far,
Yet God will bring him where the Blessed are."

**Man is conscious mind or spirit; this stands** for his
objective faculty. The objective mind of man is his
recognition of life in a conscious state . . it is the only
attribute of man that is volitional, or self-choosing.
Consequently, it is the spiritual man. The conscious mind of
man is the contemplator. Let us bear in mind what we have
already learned: that the Universe is the result of the
contemplation of the Divine Mind, or the Holy Spirit, which is
God. God creates by contemplating His own I AMness, and
this contemplation, through Law, becomes the objectification
of the Self-Realization of the Infinite Mind. The Divine Nature
is reenacted in man; he is conscious mind and spirit, and, as
he contemplates, he reflects his thought into the Universal
Subjectivity where it is received and acted upon. As Mind, or
Soul, accepts these images of thought, It operates upon
unformed substance and causes it to take definite form as
body, which is unconscious form. It becomes definite form,
but the form itself is unconscious, because it is made of
immaterial substance. Body, of itself, without Mind, has
neither consciousness nor volition. Devoid of mentality, the
body neither thinks, sees, hears, feels, touches nor tastes.
Take the mentality away from a body and it becomes a
corpse. Having no conscious intelligence, it at once begins to
disintegrate and to resolve into the Universal Substance, or
unformed matter, from which it came.

**We do well to pay heed to the sayings** of the great teachers who have taught that all power is in the "I AM," and to accept this teaching by faith in their bare authority rather than not accept it at all; but the more excellent way is to know why they taught thus, and to realize for ourselves this first great law which all the masterminds have realized throughout the ages. It is indeed true that the "lost word" is the one most familiar to us, ever in our hearts and on our lips. We have lost, not the word, but the realization of its power. And as the infinite depths of meaning which the words I AM carry with them open out to us, we begin to realize the stupendous truth that we are ourselves the very power which we seek.

**When a great teacher said,** "Go into your closet and shut the door," I am sure that he meant go into your mind. Take your attention off the world, off your individual world and the collective world. Begin to explore the depths. No wonder it has been said that the kingdom of heaven . . I AM . . is in man, because those depths on the inside of consciousness are the most satisfying, the most refreshing that you will ever know. They are the key to achieving your potential.

**We have learned that the discovery** of God has to be linked up inevitably with Self discovery, that the Universe in which we live is spiritual and not material, that there is only One Mind, to which time and space are nothing, and that this Mind of God is really our Mind. We learned, too, that there is one Substance . . the Substance of our own mind . . which is always active in the soul and ready to take form on the surface. Since the whole process through which the I AM works is one of consciousness, one must look to consciousness for everything needful in his life. Man is solely dependent upon himself . . upon his own consciousness and the power of his own Mind. He becomes masterful to the degree that he is able to harmonize his consciousness with his own divine Mind and to recognize that Mind is the Substance of all things. Mind does not become things; It is things.

**When Jesus says, "I AM the Truth,"** he is not referring to himself as a man, but to the Principle which he teaches. "I AM" means Pure Being, Life, Awareness, Consciousness, or The Unconditioned One. Our "I AMness" is God. "I AM all things to all men." This Formless Awareness becomes that which man conceives It to be; this is the law of believing . . the corner stone of life which the world rejects. When we read the word, "Verily, Verily," it means stop, look, and listen! To be born again means a spiritual rebirth . . the birth of God in man.

## BE STILL AND KNOW THAT I AM GOD"

To many who are not familiar with our thinking, this statement, applied to an individual, is considered blasphemous. But as we interpret it, there is a Divine creative center in each and every one of us. When we say, "Be still and know that I AM God," we mean that I AM the potential, I AM the creativity, I AM the possibility, I AM That which shall be. I AM not that which was. People of wisdom measure themselves in terms of today and the future. But average persons measure themselves in terms of the past. Ask them to describe their lives and they describe life entirely in terms of the past. Go to a creative mind and say: "Tell me about your life." He or she describes what they are doing right now, not what they did years ago. They talk about what they are doing now and what they are expecting to do. That's creativity. That's a now person in a now experience, creating something greater in the period to come. That is a person who knows he has a success mechanism and is using it. Such a person has accepted himself as he is, not as he was. You are what you are, and that is good. You can direct it. You can become more of it. You can experience its benefits. That's what we are trying to do. We are trying definitely, with intent and purpose, to have health, to have ease, to have order, to have peace within ourselves, to have self-expression, and to have loving relationships with others. We can have all of these because all of the equipment necessary is already within us. We do not plead to a deity for what we want. We are it. We do not beseech the gates of heaven, because your next thought is the gate of heaven.

**When you say, "I AM" that is God.** We do not speak of God to come. God is here already . . your own I AMness . . the Eternal Now. Accept your good now; unite with your desire in consciousness. Enter into the finished state of accomplishment. Let your psychological time-clock be, "It is done!" "It is finished!" Never say, "Oh, next year business will be better." The time the average man speaks of means his relationship to earth in its diurnal motion, and the position of the sun; it means his relationship to the events of today and tomorrow. Prolonged desire and failure to realize your heart's desires give rise to frustration, illness, and neurosis. The ideal, the desire of your heart exists now. It is the concrete living reality in the next dimension of mind. Remember that thoughts are things. Recognize the power of your thought; it is supreme in your life. Go within now, and enter into the mental atmosphere that your prayers are answered . . your dreams are fulfilled. Accept your good now. Say from your heart, the thing I AM seeking already exists, otherwise, I could not even desire it. I accept the fulfillment of my desire completely now, and I rest in the conviction that "It is done." "Now is the accepted time." I accept my good now . . not in some future day. I give thanks for it now . . this moment . . and enter into the joy of the answered prayer.

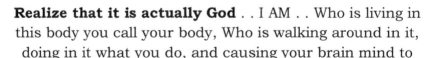

**Realize that it is actually God** . . I AM . . Who is living in this body you call your body, Who is walking around in it, doing in it what you do, and causing your brain mind to think and your mouth to say what you think and say.

**On another memorable occasion** Jesus declared again that the I AM is the enduring principle of Life. It is this that is the Resurrection and the Life; not, as Martha supposed, a new principle to be infused from without at some future time, but an inherent core of vitality awaiting only its own recognition of itself to triumph over death and the grave. And yet, again hear the Master's answer to the inquiring Thomas. How many of us, like him, desire to know the way! To hear of wonderful powers latent in man and requiring only development is beautiful and hopeful, if we could only find out the way to develop them; but who will show us the way? The answer comes with no uncertain note. The I AM includes everything. It is at once "the Way, the Truth, and the Life": not the Life only, or the Truth only, but also the Way by which to reach them. Can words be plainer? It is by continually affirming and relying on the I AM in ourselves as identical with the I AM That is the One and Only Life, whether manifested or unmanifested, in all places of the universe, that we shall find the way to the attainment of all Truth and of all Life. Here we have the predicate which we are seeking to complete our affirmation regarding ourselves. I AM . . what? the Three things which include all things: Truth, which is all Knowledge and Wisdom; Life, which is all Power and Love; and the unfailing Way which will lead us step by step, if we follow it, to heights too sublime and environment too wide for our present juvenile imaginings to picture.

**What we know about Subjective Mind** proves that It is unconscious of time, knows neither time nor process. It knows only the completion, the answer. That is why it is written, "Before they call, I will answer." Cosmic Creation is from idea to object. It does not know anything about process; process is involved in it but not consciously. Correct practice should know that ultimate right action is now, today. If we say, "Tomorrow it is going to be," then according to the very law we are using we hold the answer in a state of FUTURITY WHICH CAN NEVER BECOME PRESENT. If a gardener holds his seed in his hand and says, "Tomorrow I AM going to plant this seed," his garden will never start growing. Therefore, Jesus said: "When ye pray, believe that ye have and ye shall receive." He did not say believe and you will immediately have. He said, "Ye shall receive." He did not deny the natural law of evolution and growth. Nature operates according to a law of logical sequence.

**God is consciousness and awareness** and order and design and knowledge and intelligence and spirit. He is infinite. He cannot know himself as infinity, but only by becoming something finite. Thus God seeks to expand His sense of Self by becoming things, and each thing says, "I AM this." What you believe yourself to be is what you believe God to be. The limitations and lacks you impose upon yourself you impose upon I AM. No one can possibly believe there is any limitation on I AM, thus the magnificent truth is that there is no limitation on any man.

### Defining Prosperity

**The individual is his own prosperity.** I AM my own prosperity. You are your own prosperity. So let us define what we mean by that term. Prosperity is the freedom to do what you want to do when you want to do it. Most people think of prosperity in terms of money. Having all the money you need is very important. However, as you go along, you will find that such things as health, love, and creative ideas also play a part in the definition: Prosperity is the freedom to do what you want to do when you want to do it. How do you achieve this freedom? Perhaps your earnings are low or you may even be temporarily unemployed. How do you go about achieving the prosperity that may seem far beyond your reach?

You do it by what I call profitable thinking. By thinking what you want, you stop thinking what you don't want. Gradually, what you don't want slips away, and in its place that which you want begins to happen. We know that the subconscious mind takes what you give it, and produces it. One of the great things that we now understand is that the subconscious mind is totally impersonal. Your subconscious mind takes what you give it and assumes that what you give it is what you want. Your deliberate thinking . . what I call your intention thinking . . is a spiritual tool that you use to bring abundance into your life. You use your feelings . . your emotions . . as you think with intent, with purpose, and with plan in order to cause any object or event that you desire to materialize. You can demonstrate only that which you hold steadfastly in your (I AM) consciousness.

**This unconditioned consciousness, the I AM,** is that
knowing reality in whom all conditioned states – conceptions
of myself – begin and end, but which ever remains the
unknown knowing being when all the known ceases to be. All
that I have ever believed myself to be, all that I now believe
myself to be, and all that I shall ever believe myself to be, are
but attempts to know myself . . the unknown, undefined
reality. This unknown knowing one, or unconditioned
consciousness, is my true being, the one and only reality. I
AM the unconditioned reality conditioned as that which I
believe myself to be. I AM the believer limited by my beliefs,
the knower defined by the known. The world is my
conditioned consciousness objectified. That which I feel and
believe to be true of myself is now projected in space as my
world. The world . . my mirrored self . . ever bears witness of
the state of consciousness in which I live.

**God is unity; man is diversity.** United, they manifest
harmony, the true expression of the Silence. The soul is the
constant expression of the I AM. It is the same whether
Universal or individual. Heaven and harmony mean the same
thing; when we work and think in harmony, all our action is
constructive.

**We can raise world-thought to a higher level.** Not only can
we banish within ourselves conditions but we can become as
the Master did, banishing that which is in others by the
Power of the Word. And what is the Power of the Word? "And
the Word was with God, and the Word was God, and the
Word was made flesh." That is the Word. The Word was with
God, the Word was God and the Word is God and the Word is
made flesh. I AM the Word! I AM is the WORD. "I AM shall be
My Name for all time. Go and tell my people that I AM has
sent you." "I AM" in God is identical in man. But man does
not know it, therefore he has to come to the Fountain before
he can drink. And the "I AM" expresses itself in Perfection
when the individual realizes perfection and recognizes it as
the Infinite Expression in himself and through himself and
as the very foundation of his being.

The Consciousness of God is the one Consciousness in all
humanity, each and every one of us is an individualization of
that Infinite Consciousness. It is therefore perfectly clear that
my consciousness and your consciousness have the same
source. The Divine Consciousness is our foundation and is
perfect. When your consciousness, this silent self, becomes
aware of itself then it begins to externalize itself because
there is no other Substance except the Substance of God:
there is no other Intelligence except the Active Principle of
Life which manifests the Divine Image, which is man.

**Just imagine yourself surrounded by mind,** so plastic, so receptive, that it receives the slightest impression of your thought. Whatever you think it takes up and executes for you. Every thought is received and acted upon. Not some but all thoughts. Whatever the pattern we provide, that will be our demonstration. If we cannot get over thinking that we are poor then we will still remain poor. As soon as we become rich in our thought then we will be rich in our expression. These are not mere words, but the deepest truth that has ever come to the human race. Hundreds of thousands of the most intelligent thinkers and the most spiritual people of our day are proving this truth.

We are not dealing with illusions but with realities; pay no more attention to the one who ridicules these ideas than you would to the blowing of the wind. In the center of your own soul choose what you want to become, to accomplish; keep it to yourself. Every day in the silence of absolute conviction know that it is now done. It is just as much done, as far as you are concerned, as it will be when you experience it in the outer. Imagine yourself to be what you want to be. See only that which you desire, refuse even to think of the other. Stick to it, never doubt. Say many times a day, "I AM That thing," realize what this means. It means that the great Universal power of Mind is that, and it cannot fail.

**Our first step in demonstration is to contact God.** We then have the fullness of God's wisdom, love and truth (or power, substance and intelligence) with us in bringing it forth. Our work is to begin from the I AM in us which is one with the I AM That is in all, and all in all. A leaf on a vine begins its expression at that point within itself wherein it is joined to the whole vine . . its stem. This is the door through which the expression of the vine comes forth into the leaf. Even so within us is the "door," the Christ within, the I AM in our consciousness which contacts the great I AM That is the life and light of all.

Your expression is to be given forth from within you, even as the leaf unfolds from within itself. Your affairs are to be operated from within you. "But thou, when thou prayest, enter into thy closet (the inner sanctuary of the soul) and when thou hast shut thy door, pray to thy Father which is in secret; and thy Father which seeth in secret shall reward thee openly." The first and greatest commandment, the Master said, is this important thing of making complete at-one-ment with the Father within.

He gave it in the following words:

"Thou shalt love the Lord thy God with all thy heart, with all thy soul, with all thy strength and with all thy mind."

Do you not see how you must be centered in the I AM within you, drawing the whole of your good from him, and that every force of your nature is to operate from the divine self? "In the beginning" of all expression is God, the God within, else God could not be expressed, or brought forth.

**Through each of us God attains self-consciousness,** and each of us is God incarnate. In our lives we accept the limitations of the flesh and the inhibitions of the ego, and thus we fall short of God-consciousness. We ask ourselves where we have come from and where we are going, for we have lost the remembrance of having always been, just as we cannot see that we will always be. The development of our ego thrusts upon us a precarious duality of mind, wherein Conscious Mind over-runs Universal Subconscious Mind, and we come to regard ourselves as ego only, instead of universal Self which we truly are. "How can God possibly be the poor thing that I AM?" a man will ask himself, identifying himself with ego and failing to perceive that he is consciousness only. Free yourself from the bonds of the ego, and you will forget the poor thing that you thought you were, and become one with God.

**"My mind is a center of Divine operation.** The Divine operation is always for expansion and fuller expression, and this means the production of something beyond what has gone before, something entirely new, not included in past experience, though proceeding out of it by an orderly sequence of growth. Therefore, since the Divine cannot change its inherent nature, it must operate in the same manner in me; consequently in my own special world, of which I AM the center, it will move forward to produce new conditions, always in advance of any that have gone before."

**You must separate yourself** from all your external faculties, from your mind, from your body, because they are but instruments that you use. The Consciousness must analyze everything external to itself. When you say "I AM," realize that it is the Real. The "I AM" enables you to move, think, act; and you are using your instruments as a means of expression.

**We have a right to choose what we shall induce** in Mind. The way in which our thoughts are to become manifest, we cannot always see . . or should we be disturbed that we do not see the way . . because effect is potential in cause. "I AM Alpha and Omega" and all that comes between cause and effect. Cause and effect are really one, and if we have a given cause set in motion, the effect will have to equal the cause. One is the inside and the other the outside of the same thing. A certain, specific, intelligent idea in Mind, will produce a certain, specific, concrete manifestation equal to itself. There is One Infinite Principle, One Infinite Thought-Stuff, One Infinite Creative Power, but countless numbers of forms, which change as the specific idea behind them changes.

**I AM a creative being. I create by thinking** ideas and at the same time knowing that there is a Force at my disposal which is universal, wise, and loving in its nature. I choose my ideas and think them. The Force brings them forth. I can create as much as I can think.

**Subjectivity is entirely receptive and neutral** as we have learned, and It can take our thoughts only the way we think them . . It has no alternative. If I say, "I AM unhappy," and continue to say it, the subconscious mind says, "Yes, you are unhappy," and keeps me unhappy as long as I say it, for thoughts are things, and an active thought will provide an active condition for good or evil. Suppose one has thought poverty year after year, he has thereby personified a law which continues to perpetuate this condition. If the thought is not erased the condition will remain. A law has been set in motion which says "I AM poor," and sees to it that this is so. This is at first an autosuggestion, then it becomes an unconscious memory, working day and night. This is what decides how the Law of Attraction works for us, because the laws of attraction and repulsion are entirely subjective. Our use of them may be conscious to start with, but it becomes subconscious as soon as used.

**Your Consciousness enables you to speak,** breathe, walk, talk, etc., and the Intelligence fulfils the act. The Consciousness directs the motion, and the Intelligence completes it. You see the manifestation of Nature, you do not see Nature herself; you do not see Intelligence, but you see the action of Intelligence . . or the energy resulting from the action, which is the form in Substance. The Substance is, and always will be, perfect in itself, although the form might not be perfect. "According to your faith so be it unto you." "Be ye perfect as your Father in Heaven is perfect." This really means that in the Divine Consciousness . . the Perfect Image exists.

If you have perfect faith, the Perfect Intelligence will express the Perfect Image in the Perfect Substance by its own perfect action. This is the true Law of Life as taught by Jesus Himself. It is not the Substance you have to change, nor the Consciousness, nor the Intelligence, but the form that you created in the Substance. Do you understand? This is very deep, but very simple. When you understand this you will never again be lost in dogma, creed nor philosophy. It does not matter one iota whether they are true or not true. The essential thing is this, GOD IS and I AM . . YOU ARE. Through faith and belief we transcend our experiences and the experiences of others, and enter into the realm of Divine Action, where all is possible.

**"As the spirit of good (God).** There is a consciousness within man ever affirming: I AM Love, I AM Spirit, Truth, Wisdom, Knowledge and Power, all expressing in the one manifestation Love." "Is it possible to comprehend love?" "We can neither see nor comprehend that mysterious something man terms love." "How can man direct, control and express his latent forces?" "By a wise understanding of nature's laws, and a consciousness that he possesses all power, and as he progresses along the path he will recognize the finer vibrations; and in time the exoteric plane will fade from view and its place will be filled with spiritual truths, in the midst of which he lives and has his being."

"How can he attain this spiritual attitude?" "By intelligently directing the One creative power, Thought" the ability to think and to be that which he thinks." "Is there any law in nature which will aid in this spiritual development?" "Yes; the Law of affirmation and suggestion. A wise understanding of these Laws will make man a master who will proclaim his own fate."

**The "I AM" is both individual and universal,** that is, the individual "I" is part of the Universal "I AM." The "I AM consciousness" means that part of thought, both conscious and subjective, which not only affirms its unity with God, but which also understands the meaning of its affirmation.

**There is a Force everywhere about** and within you. This Force is infinite, universal, all-loving and wise, all-powerful, alive, full of life, life itself. Think to yourself . . I AM. I live and am quite definitely myself. I can create. I do my creating through my thinking. I AM a thinker. This Force moves according to my thinking, pushes my idea forth into form. The more faith, determination, persistence, harmony, good will, reverence, and gratitude I feel, the better this Force is able to push my hopes and aspirations toward fulfillment. I would be all I can be. I can be as much as I can think. I must deliberately make the effort to think the best, highest, finest, biggest that I can. My thinking frees me from my difficulties.

**The Substance of the Great "I AM"** is the perfect Substance out of which all things are made, brought forth by Consciousness and Intelligence in the Substance. This perfect Substance is the foundation of and supports all forms. In the Consciousness the Divine Idea exists; the Intelligence completes the Idea in detail, and the Idea is expressed in the Substance in all planes of manifestation, including the spiritual, mental, astral and physical planes, each being but a modification of the one above it. Substance having no power of its own, changes, fulfilling the expression of the Intelligence directed by the Consciousness. God is all there is . . Consciousness, Intelligence and Substance. God is expressing Himself through the particular center of Consciousness that you are. Everything is given form by consciousness . . your consciousness is the Consciousness of God. It is the realization of this that enables you to say "I and the Father are one."

**We express as much of God as we intelligently** know of Him; and it is our daily duty to use the God-power He has invested in us to express Him in the highest form we know, by every word, deed, action and thought; and by loving all humanity, of which we are a part. Every time we fail to do this, all of humanity fails; and every time we progress, all of humanity progresses . . because there is but One.

If we have health, happiness, love and prosperity, we are expressing God. If we have disease, unhappiness, jealousy and poverty, we are not expressing the highest we are capable of; therefore, we are not expressing God intelligently.

To express the highest of anything, we must first know and understand the lowest operative part of that thing or condition. Knowing this, we must set to work and separate the low from the high, or the good from the evil; and to do this intelligently, we must first know what is really good and what is really evil; and this knowledge is only gained by coining into a higher and more understandable consciousness of what God is; and then to work from that point . . knowing that God is your Higher Self and your physical body is your child. You are the master of it, the body; or, it is the master of you, the thinker. Which is it with you? Which is the master?

If you have meditated correctly, as I have explained to you, on the I AM, or the God within; you will know which is the master . . you, the thinker, or your physical body. When you are positive that you, the thinker, have complete control over all of your physical and material desires, sensations and emotions, then, and only then, are you the master.

**There is nothing greater than Truth;** nothing can destroy Truth; no philosophy, dogma nor creed can limit Truth. Perhaps through dogma, philosophy or creeds you have reached this stage; but they were only stepping stones . . or =perhaps they were limitations because you thought them the final word. Perhaps you studied occultism and you thought this was the true law; and you thought this was the only way to go. You perhaps have studied Eastern Philosophy, Yoga, etc. They have been stepping stones, but now we have the Truth. The Truth is Infinity, and there is nothing greater. There is nothing but Infinity; what man sees as evil is in his mind or in the mind of others.

There is only one Substance, one Consciousness, one Intelligence, and that is all there is; all forms are created out of these "Three in One" and are expressions . . all united, all in one, and one in all. Therefore, who are you? Who am I? I AM That I AM, I AM the Consciousness, the Intelligence, the Substance. I AM That I AM. I cannot be anything else; it is impossible for me to be more or less. If I try to be, I AM imaging, creating concepts in my mind; what I believe seems true to me, but it may be false. The Infinite Being is all there is, is present everywhere, is all Power there is, all Intelligence there is, all Substance there is. Then I and the Father must be one . . are one. It is a self-evident truth; it speaks for itself and no one can deny it . . but science is not sure.

**The Life-principle is always the same.** It is always the principle of confident Affirmation in the calm knowledge that all things are but manifestations of itself, and that, therefore, all must move together in one mighty unity which admits of no discordant elements. This "unity of the spirit" once clearly grasped, to say I AM is to send the vibrations of our thought-currents throughout the universe to do our bidding when and where we will; and, conversely, it is to draw in the vitalizing influences of Infinite Spirit as from a boundless ocean of Life, which can never be exhausted and from which no power can hold us back.

And all this is so because it is the supreme law of Nature. It is not the introduction of a new order, but simply the allowing of the original and only possible order to flow on to its legitimate fulfillment. A Divine Order, truly, but nowhere shall we find anything that is not Divine; and it is to the realization of this Divine and Living Order that it is the purpose of the Bible to lead us. But we shall never realize it around us until we first realize it within us. We can see God outside only by the light of God inside; and this light increases in proportion as we become conscious of the Divine nature of the innermost I AM which is the center of our own individuality.

**Your unconditioned consciousness,** or I AM, and that which you are conscious of being, are one.

**Minds centered upon the cares of the world,** and busy with the small duties of life, need to be opened by study and contemplation to the grandeur of the great God whose marvelous presence is manifest in all the laws and forms of the universe. Students should seek that instruction which opens the mind to the mighty spirit of life. This is necessary, that the mind may receive new life and the power to manifest life in endless abundance. Says the voice of truth: "I AM come that ye might have life, and have it more abundantly." The truth reveals the life which was always here but which we did not recognize. And our recognition opens up our mind to receive of its blessing. Recognition grows into faith, and faith builds up the mental forces that polarize life.

**The answer to every question is within man,** because man is within Spirit, and Spirit is an Indivisible Whole! The solution to every problem is within man; the healing of all disease is within man; the forgiveness of all sin is within man; the raising of the dead is within man; Heaven is within man. This is why Jesus prayed to this indwelling "I AM" and said: "Our Father which art in Heaven," and again he said: "The Kingdom of Heaven is within you."

**There are two degrees of this consciousness,** the first of which we will term the realization of the "I", a consciousness of "I" AM . . a something which causes one to know he lives and has his being, independent of the physical body, a state in which all doubts of man's immortality are at once swept away, and he feels himself lifted up and away from this material plane to a life of sunshine and joy.

The second decree is the consciousness of, All life is One life and "I" AM that life, the "I" AM consciousness, which causes the pupil to recognize his oneness with the Universal Whole. "I" AM the highest manifestation of God's expression.

This awakening is the consciousness that, among all the worlds . . suns and planets known and unknown to civilized man, "I" AM the highest expression thereof. The unfolding of this "I" AM life will enable the student to become Master and to solve the great secrets of the External Universe.

**Man's consciousness is God,** his I AM. I AM conscious of the state. I AM the father-mother of all my ideas and my mind remains faithful to this new concept of self. My mind is disciplined. I take into that state the disciples, and I shut out of that state everything that would deny it.

## Neville Goddard interprets "Jehovah"

**The first thing you must discover if you would unlock the secret** of the Bible, is the meaning of the symbolic name of the creator which is known to all as Jehovah. This word "Jehovah" is composed of the four Hebrew letters – JOD HE VAU HE. The whole secret of creation is concealed within this name.

The first letter, JOD, represents the absolute state or consciousness unconditioned; the sense of undefined awareness; that all inclusiveness out of which all creation or conditioned states of consciousness come.

In the terminology of today JOD is I AM, or unconditioned consciousness.

The second letter, HE, represents the only begotten Son, a desire, an imaginary state. It symbolizes an idea; a defined subjective state or clarified mental picture.

The third letter, VAU, symbolizes the act of unifying or joining the conceiver (JOD), the consciousness desiring to the conception (HE), the state desired, so that the conceiver and the conception become one.

Fixing a mental state, consciously defining yourself as the state desired, impressing upon yourself the fact that you are now that which you imagined or conceived as your objective, is the function of VAU. It nails or joins the consciousness desiring to the thing desired. The cementing or joining process is accomplished subjectively by feeling the reality of that which is not yet objectified.

The fourth letter, HE, represents the objectifying of this subjective agreement. The JOD HE VAU makes man or the manifested world (HE), in the image and likeness of itself, the subjective conscious state. So the function of the final HE is to objectively bear witness to the subjective state JOD HE VAU.

Conditioned consciousness continually objectifies itself on the screen of space. The world is the image and likeness of the subjective conscious state which created it.

The visible world of itself can do nothing; it only bears record of its creator, the subjective state. It is the visible Son (HE) bearing witness of the invisible Father, Son and Mother . . JOD HE VAU . . a Holy Trinity which can only be seen when made visible as man or manifestation.

Your unconditioned consciousness (JOD) is your I AM which visualizes or imagines a desirable state (HE), and then becomes conscious of being that state imagined by feeling and believing itself to be the imagined state. The conscious union between you who desire and that which you desire to be, is made possible through the VAU, or your capacity to feel and believe.

Believing is simply living in the feeling of actually being the state imagined . . by assuming the consciousness of being the state desired. The subjective state symbolized as JOD HE VAU then objectifies itself as HE, thereby completing the mystery of the creator's name and nature, JOD HE VAU HE (Jehovah).

JOD is to be aware; HE is to be aware of something; VAU is to be aware as, or to be aware of being that which you were only aware of. The second HE is your visible objectified world which is made in the image and likeness of the JOD HE VAU, or that which you are aware of being.

"And God said, Let Us make man in Our image, after Our likeness". Let us, JOD HE VAU make the objective manifestation (HE) in our image, the image of the subjective state.

The world is the objectified likeness of the subjective conscious state in which consciousness abides. This understanding that consciousness is the one and only reality is the foundation of the Bible.

The stories of the Bible are attempts to reveal in symbolic language the secret of creation as well as to show man the one formula to escape from all of his own creations.

This is the true meaning of the name of Jehovah, the name by which all things are made and without which there is nothing made that is made.

First, you are aware; then you become aware of something; then you become aware as that which you were aware of; then you behold objectively that which you are aware of being.

**We let go of everything, drop every fear from our minds**, drop all confusion from our thought, and enter into the inner secret communion with that great Reality, which is our Universal Self . . God . . in Whom we live and move and have our being. We are conscious that this Divine Presence overshadows and indwells. It is both without this physical, mental being and within this physical, mental being. Therefore, It is the spiritual Reality of this being, the I AM, which is Universal, Eternal, and Perfect.

**Until one is poised in the I AM Consciousness** so that one always sees through the eyes of Love, the imperfections of another stand forth more or less glaringly, thus distracting the attention and preventing one from seeing the good in the other. But when we have given ourselves and all of our personal ideas wholly over to the Loving One within, He gradually frees us from such separative forces and permits us a glimpse of Himself in the souls of others.

Those favored ones who are vouchsafed such glimpse ever afterward cannot help but keep their hearts wide open, letting His love pour out when contacting others, ever seeking and longing to see Him again in all the souls they meet. Of course the knowledge of God being all there is must become a fixed part of our consciousness, in order to cause us thus always to seek to see and know the Christ-self of our brother. It is magical in effect when one really looks for good in another . . one can always find it; when one really seeks to know God, in one way or another He will surely reveal Himself.

**We must stop driving the rightful heritage** of our prosperity from us by making lack a reality. Every time we say: "I AM demonstrating over lack, just what have we really said? We have admitted the reality of lack; for . . if we did not believe there was a lack of something, why should we try to overcome lack? Therefore, instead of talking and thinking lack, we should talk and think prosperity; and then we shall have prosperity. If everyone capable of thinking, would think and talk prosperity for a week, we would have so much prosperity we would not be able to control it.

**I AM a creative being.** There is a mighty and intelligent
Force about and within me which runs for me according to
my thinking. I can have anything I AM able to think. I can
create a new body, new conditions, by changing my ideas,
my images, by getting new ideas and images and calling to
the Force.

**"I AM the light of the world."** Jesus was not referring to his
human personality, but to the Principle inherent in generic
man. They who follow this inner Principle shall have the light
of life; for this Principle is life. "I AM" has a dual meaning. It
is both individual and universal. God was revealed to Moses
as the great "I AM," the Universal Cause, the Causeless or
Self-existent One. Moses taught that "I AM" is the First
Principle of all life, and the Law of cause and effect running
through everything.

The whole teaching of Moses is based upon the perception of
this "First Principle." Jesus said that he came, not to destroy
the law of Moses, but to fulfill it. How could he fulfill it except
by teaching the relationship of the universal "I AM" to the
individual "I"? In all the sayings of Jesus, we find this
thought brought out: that God is Universal Spirit and man is
His image and likeness ... an individualization of His eternity.
Therefore, when we understand our own "I" we shall walk in
that light which lights the world unto the perfect "I AM."

**Still mind, be still; let God within you speak:** I AM That I AM. Still the mind, and allow the perfect concept to be brought forth by God within. Still the personal mind. I AM . . GOD. Be still, I AM God within. You then blend the greater with the smaller, and the outer becomes inner, and the inner becomes outer . . both blended together. God is all there is . . visible and invisible; and we are one with Him. It is our belief in separation from Him that causes sin, poverty, sickness and death.

Realize that heaven is a perfect state of consciousness, and that hell is the reverse. "Be ye perfect as your Father in heaven is perfect." Therefore hell does not exist in reality, it only exists as a false concept in the mind of man, and you have it here if you accept it. God created all, filling the world with light. "Let there be light" is the spoken word of Life, because Divine Consciousness exists in life and can express itself in any degree.

**To desire is to confess that you do not now possess what you** desire, and because all things are yours, you rob yourself by living in the state of desire.

My savior is my desire.

As I want something I AM looking into the eyes of my savior.

But if I continue wanting it, I deny my Jesus, my savior, for as I want I confess I AM not and "except ye believe that I AM He ye die in your sins."

I cannot have and still continue to desire what I have. I may enjoy it, but I cannot continue wanting it.

**It is not easy to attain SELF MASTERY;** for each day and hour there are pitfalls in our path . . trials and tribulations waiting to conquer us and make us slaves of self, if we do not overcome them.

The most effective way to master self, is to pray as David did in the Nineteenth Psalm: "Cleanse Thou me from secret faults. Keep bade Thy servant also from presumptuous sins; let them not have dominion over me."

If we beseech God to give us dominion over ourselves; and then we realize and use the Infinite Power of God within us, we shall not only attain SELF MASTERY, but every good thing for our peace, prosperity, health and happiness . . now and always.

How truly blessed are those who can say:

"It matters not how strait the gate,
How charged the punishment with scroll,
I AM the master of my fate:
I AM the captain of my soul."

**He told them to believe in God, and because of their belief** in God, to believe also in him. Again he is referring to the individual "I" as the outward manifestation of the Universal "I AM." We are to believe in ourselves because we believe in God. The two are ONE. We are to know that passing events cannot hinder the onward march of the soul. The temporal imperfection of the human cannot dim the eternal integrity of the Divine.

## WHO IS "I?"

**Ask yourself who this observer is that you refer to as "I."**
It is not thought. It is not body. It simply is, has being,
observes. In the contemplative sense in which you feel it
now, it is neither past nor present nor future, but simply
exists. I AM. I observe. I decide.

Here is your true being. Here is your real Self, the unfettered,
untrammeled, eternal spectator. To find this point of
consciousness from which all things and thoughts and
moods are a matter of observation is to find the spiritual
center of gravity, is to know yourself in all your true freedom
and joy. This "I," this observer, is the indwelling God, the real
Self, the personal consciousness that is in all things and all
life.

**If I can deny the limitations of my birth**, my environment,
and the belief that I am but an extension of my family tree,
and feel within myself that I AM Christ, and sustain this
assumption until it takes a central place and forms the
habitual center of my energy, I will do the works attributed to
Jesus. Without thought or effort I will mold a world in
harmony with that perfection which I have assumed and feel
springing within me.

**There is a Universal force for me to use.** This force can create for me what I desire. I take my thought from the idea of the trouble I am in. I go within the chamber of my mind. I close the doors of sight, sound, taste, touch, smell for the time being.

I think as a decree. I order it, but order it lovingly with a feeling of good will. The force then obeys my Decree. I AM using my equipment, my creative equipment. Nothing can bind me. I AM a free creative being. I AM divine in nature. I AM living close to my God who is present with me as a universal force in my life.

I need no longer be bound to lack. I AM living with the idea of plenty. The force of God is present everywhere now. It brings forth my idea into form, into my world. God the Good is all there is. I AM like him. I AM like him in essence and in attributes, in qualities. The more I look upon Him, the more I think about Him, the more I grow like Him, the more I call upon Him, the more response I receive. There can be no response unless there be first the call.

I AM thinking my idea . . SUCCESS, HEALTH, INCREASE, POSITION . . while calling or looking toward the universal God-force within and about me. Because of this unity with the Force I AM bringing forth my idea into its outer, concrete form.

I AM careful. I must watch the trend of my thinking, for the trend of my thinking makes a great difference in the results. The trend of my thinking is the setting of my idea. Just as the setting of a precious stone influences the whole, so my general trend of thinking influences the outcome of my idea which I would create. I AM a free soul in God. I create as high as I can think.

**The inner force of the thought, when awakened,** will express and produce the exact nature of the thought; and therefore, whatever you may wish your thought to produce, if you think the right thought and think living thought, the results will come as expected. To think the right thought is simple; all that is necessary for general purposes is to affirm that you are what you wish to realize and express through body, mind and personality, and to form in the mind as clear a mental picture as possible of those conditions you desire to produce in yourself. If you wish to produce health affirm mentally, "I AM well", "I AM strong", "I AM strong and well", "I AM perfectly whole and sound through and through", "Absolute health fills and thrills every atom in my being", and statements of a similar nature. Think these thoughts over and over again with deep conviction until your mind is actually full of them; and at the same time picture mentally the condition of health in every part of your system.

**You do not have to worry about getting there** by this route or that route; you are already there but do not know it. No longer will you have to believe that which is false to receive the Truth. You are filled with the Truth when you know it. No one can create the Truth. IT IS. Only false concepts we create. The Truth is beyond our imagination, therefore what we have in our imagination is an idea . . a sensation; the Truth is none of these. IT IS. You are the Truth. "I AM the Truth," the Master said.

**Of one thing we may be certain;** it is possible to remember anything that has ever transpired on this planet. It is also possible to see what might happen in the future, except it is changed through prayer. The real truth about you is this: I am referring to the Eternal You . . the I AMness within you, your own Consciousness, or Awareness. You have been all men who ever lived, who live now, or whoever will live. You have been Jesus, Moses, Beethoven, Lincoln, and Shakespeare. Your Consciousness or awareness has played all roles; It has been everywhere; It has seen everything . . all is within It . . even the whole universe is within your own I AMness. Your Consciousness or Awareness wrote all Bibles, and spoke all languages; therefore you . . the Invisible Self of you . . knows the meaning of every part of the Bible. Ask yourself what did I mean when I wrote the Bible two thousand or five thousand years ago? The Deep Self of you has the answer.

**Jesus concluded the prayer with the oldest** word in our possession. Amen. The word is actually the sacred name for the Power back of all creation and means literally, The Hidden One. Amen is really the cohesive force of any prayer. It is a word that precipitates immediate expression. It clinches and vitalizes all other affirmations. It sets the Universal Forces into activity. Amen should be used after every affirmation and prayer, and be thought of as the Power of the I AM (Spirit) to impregnate substance. Amen is the mighty pronouncement that It is done.

## THE UNIVERSAL MIND ACTIVE THROUGH YOU

**We HAVE now reached the lesson** that deals with the
metaphysical aspect of our subject. First we discovered the
manner in which Mind works from the objective side. Then
we became acquainted with the idea that the world we see is
not material but spiritual. We also learned that the thought
of space is eliminated by knowing that space has never
existed. Now we are ready for the thought that Universal
Mind is active from the subjective side. Its manifestations, to
be sure, will be objective.

The student should keep in mind the fact that desire from
within is not his personal desire. The desire for health,
wealth and happiness is not personal but impersonal. The
Universal Mind desires to manifest and express these states
of Being through you. Because this is true, the personal
struggle, which is always accompanied by anxiety and worry,
may be dropped from man's life. To learn this lesson is to
have learned much.

Since desire is in the great Mind and all these desires are
good, the only thing necessary for us to do is to let. This,
remember, does not mean that there will be inaction but it
does mean that you will be conscious that it is not the
personal but the impersonal "you" that works. Relaxation of
course is necessary but when one has understanding, he
finds it easy to relax.

God is "I AM" and "I AM" . . God. When the personal mind
(conscious) relaxes and "lets" the great Mind ("I AM") at the
center of one's very Being express, it will work and work
perfectly. As you recall the teaching step by step, you will be
aware that I AM" is at the center of things. You also find that
"I AM" is at the center of your own Being. This then is plain
and reasonable . . that when you are still and your conscious

mind is conscious not of things. but of the "I AM" within you, you are in tune with everything in the Universe. Being in tune with the Universe, you exert an unconscious pull on things and will draw to you the thing which you desire most.

That is why I do not say, "Think of the thing that you want," but "Think of the Substance ("I AM") of the thing."

This great Universal Mind {"I AM") is always flowing into our bodies, whether we are conscious of it or not. The student should remember that he does not alter the fact of Truth by what he thinks of it; he simply alters his own manifestation of it. We do not change Truth by our opinions of it; we change its manifestation in our own experience. "As a man thinketh, so is he" . . in manifestation.

Inasmuch as this great Mind is flowing into our bodies, it must. of necessity have an outlet. This conclusion leads us to accept the following: The Universal Mind flows through us, but registers or localizes itself in the solar plexus and from this point radiates by thought to the world. Therefore we see that God ("I AM") is the only Thinker, Actor, Power and Life. Then "I AM" . . Success or if it would be easier for the student to realize the impersonal, he may say, "I AM is Success." If he wishes to say, "God is Success," he is saying the same thing. It is not so much what we say, so far as the words are concerned; it is the understanding with which we say them.

God is the "inflow" and God is also the "outflow"; then "God is All and in All." Since there is but one Energy and that is God, this is the only conclusion for man to reach: God speaks; God works; God thinks; God acts; God writes; God walks; God sings; God plays upon the musical instrument. I might go on indefinitely, for this power is "All and in All."

By receiving this understanding, the student will see that human "personality" is eliminated; the one who has gained this knowledge has found a new world.

Those who are conscious of God speaking, speak perfectly; those who realize that God walks, have been healed and have regained the power of walking after having been in bed for years. The realization that God sees, has cured many of the belief in faulty sight. Since "God is All and in All," there is no personal mind; no personal self; no personal desire, will or responsibility. Personal mind, self, will and desires mean belief in human personality (separation from God), and will bring failure unless corrected by a knowledge of Truth.

"Sensing the Allness of God, leaving out all trace of human personality, if earnestly engaged in, will permanently remove every difficulty from my path."

**I AM a creative being. I create by thinking ideas.** My ideas are brought forth by the wise and loving Force. I create as high as I can think. My equipment consists of mind-force with my ideas and feeling. It is wise for me to love much while I AM creating. Practice makes perfect. I will myself to practice meditation, to image the idea I wish to bring forth. I practice going into my closet of mind and closing the door. I practice living with the idea I wish to bring forth.

**Your consciousness is the individualized** Consciousness of God and the only creative Power there is. When it begins to manifest in your own mind, creating images and externalizing these images, the consciousness is still within them and is the only reality they have. There is nothing else real except consciousness that created them. Immediately you have a change of consciousness in regard to them it changes the forms. The same law and quality is the same in the Divine Mind, but is vastly different in degree; it is the same action, the same motive action. The Divine Mind being perfect in itself, God Almighty, there is no flaw or reaction.

This is beyond the comprehension of human beings, and even beyond the comprehension of the Archangels in Heaven, who are aware of their own consciousness yet they cannot analyze that consciousness because it recedes into eternity. The Divine Mind creating by its own Consciousness, expresses the image of man and there the Divine dwells in man and is the only reality in man. The Consciousness of God directs the Intelligence, the Active Principle, out picturing the Divine Image in the Substance and Form comes forth. I AM the Life! I AM the Life!

**One day man will realize that his own** I AMness is the God he has been seeking throughout the ages, and that his own sense of awareness . . his consciousness of being . . is the one and only reality.

**To remove the cause of so-called sickness** (sickness and disease are not real, for if they were they could never be changed or healed) is to change the thought from the present channel into another, no matter how much the physical body may desire attention.

We should say:

I AM well. I AM healthy; for the I AM of us, the God Principal, can never be otherwise. We should believe and know that we are well and healthy; and if we never doubt it, we shall be amazed at the wonderful results we will derive from this thought.

Every time we find our thought dwelling on the condition of sickness or disease, we should immediately change our thought to Love, Life, Health and Happiness. And if we cannot think of anything to meditate on, we should look at the great abundance of health and happiness in Nature; and there, we shall find many blessings to think about.

Thought can, and does, everything that humanity needs to have done. This being true, and we know it is true, we should use our thought to bring about the health and happiness within us.

**This thinking being that I AM,** creating with the Force, lives in a wonderful temple of body. My body is built and rebuilt by the thinking going on within it. I can create a perfect body if I will think thoughts which tend that way. With the Force, this creative and thinking being that I AM, living in the wonderful body, may have rich conditions about me, if I will think thoughts which tend to richness.

**There is One Infinite Mind** from which all things come. This Mind is through, in, and around man. It is the Only Mind there is and every time man thinks he uses It. There is One Infinite Spirit and every time man says "I AM" he proclaims It. There is One Infinite Substance and every time man moves he moves in It. There is One Infinite Law and every time man thinks he sets this Law in motion. There is One Infinite God and every time man speaks to this God, he receives a direct answer. ONE! ONE! ONE! "I AM God and there is none else." There is One Limitless Life, which returns to the thinker exactly what he thinks into It. One! One! One! "In all, over all, and through all." Talk, live, act, believe and know that you are a center in this One. All the Power there is, all the Presence there is, all the Love there is, all the Peace there is, all the Good there is, and the Only God there is, is Omnipresent. Consequently, the Infinite is in and through man and is in and through everything. "Act as though I AM and I will be."

**Faith or feeling is the secret of this appropriation.**
Through feeling, the consciousness desiring is joined to the
thing desired.

How would you feel if you were that which you desire to be?

Wear the mood, this feeling that would be yours if you were
already that which you desire to be; and in a little while you
will be sealed in the belief that you are. Then without effort
this invisible state will objectify itself; the invisible will be
made visible.

If you had the faith of a grain of mustard seed you would this
day through the magical substance of feeling seal yourself in
the consciousness of being that which you desire to be.

In this mental stillness or tomb-like state you would remain,
confident that you need no one to roll away the stone, for all
the mountains, stones and inhabitants of earth are nothing
in your sight. That which you now recognize to be true of
yourself (this present conscious state) will do according to its
nature among all the inhabitants of earth, and none can stay
its hand or say unto it, "What doest Thou?". None can stop
this conscious state in which you are sealed from embodying
itself, nor question its right to be.

This conscious state when properly sealed by faith is a Word
of God, I AM, for the man so seated is saying, "I AM so and
so," and the Word of God (my fixed conscious state) is spirit
and cannot return unto me void but must accomplish
whereunto it is sent. God's word (your conscious state) must
embody itself that you may know: "I AM the Lord... there is
no God beside Me"

**Therefore, it is that Jesus tells us that the I AM** is "the door." It is that central point of our individual Being which opens into the whole illimitable Life of the Infinite. If we would understand the old world precept, "know thyself," we must concentrate our thought more and more closely upon our own interior Life until we touch its central radiating point, and there we shall find that the door into the Infinite is indeed opened to us, and that we can pass from the innermost of our own Being into the innermost of All-Being. This is why Jesus spoke of "the door" as that through which we should pass in and out and find pasture. Pasture, the feeding of every faculty with its proper food, is to be found both on the within and the without. The livingness of Life consists in both concentration and externalization: it is not the dead equilibrium of inertia, but the living equilibrium of a vital and rhythmic pulsation. Involution and evolution must forever alternate, and the door of communication between them is the I AM which is the living power in both. Thus it is that the Great Affirmation is the Secret of Life, and that to say I AM with a true understanding of all that it implies is to place ourselves in touch with all the powers of the Infinite.

**I AM come that ye might have life** and have it more abundantly. The abundance that we express is always commensurate with our recognition of the Law (God). The greatest good that can come to man is the realization of the full and complete Spirit of Good within himself.

**God, within Whom all spirits exist.** The Self-Knowing One. The Conscious Universe. The Absolute. Spirit in man is that part of him which enables him to know himself. That which he really is. We do not see the spirit of man any more than we see the Spirit of God. We see what man does; but we do not see the doer. We treat of Spirit as the Active and the only Self-Conscious Principle. We define Spirit as the First Cause or God; the Universal I AM. The Spirit is Self-Propelling, It is All; It is Self-Existent and has all life within Itself. It is the Word and the Word is volition. It is Will because It chooses. It is Free Spirit because It knows nothing outside Itself, and nothing different from Itself. Spirit is the Father-Mother-God because It is the Principle of Unity back of all things. Spirit is all Life, Truth, Love, Being, Cause and Effect, and is the only Power in the Universe that knows Itself.

**As we center in the formless presence of God** and become responsive only to that which is Good, two things will happen. We shall know sensations never before experienced and shall emerge with definite guidance or leading. In praying, we talk to God and his answer comes in the form of inspiration. The voice of Intuition that speaks in the Silence is the infallible Word of God. The intuitive faculty is by far the most valuable and yet the most delicate instrument of Mind. It is the guiding force of the Soul. But unless we search for it with great patience and are obedient to its slightest prompting, we shall miss it. It is the still small voice of the I AM.

**The "I AM" is the door through which** the Consciousness, Intelligence and Substance of the Great "I AM," which is God, comes forth into expression in Form through the individual. This "I AM" Being is Consciousness, Intelligence and Substance, and is given form through Consciousness. Consciousness is the Father, Intelligence is the Mother, and the Substance is the vehicle of expression, and the Divine expression is the Child . . the Three in One. Consciousness is the Will which makes the mold and the Life Intelligence and Substance fill the mold. Consciousness directs, Intelligence fulfils the direction in the Substance, and Form comes forth; the Divine Perfect Image is expressed without effort. The Master said: "According to your faith so be it unto you." This faith is in the Consciousness, in the Perfect Divine Image; fully comprehend this and you will know the Christ Power. All things are possible to them that believe.

---

**Now I would like to step outside the limitation** of my senses but I have not yet found within myself the courage to assume I AM what these five would deny that I AM. So here I remain, conscious of my task, but without the courage to step beyond the limitations of my senses, and that which my reason denies. He tells these, "I have meat ye know not of. I AM the bread that droppeth down from heaven. I AM the wine." I know what I want to be, and because I AM That bread I feast upon it. I assume that I AM, and instead of feasting upon the fact that I am in this room talking to you and you are listening to me, and that I AM in Los Angeles, I feast upon the fact that I AM elsewhere and I walk here as though I were elsewhere. And gradually I become what I feast upon.

**It is only by a change of consciousness (I AM),** by actually changing your concept of yourself, that you can "build more stately mansions" – the manifestations of higher and higher concepts. (By manifesting is meant experiencing the results of these concepts in your world.) It is of vital importance to understand clearly just what consciousness is. The reason lies in the fact that consciousness (I AM) is the one and only reality, it is the first and only cause-substance of the phenomena of life. Nothing has existence for man save through the consciousness he has of it. Therefore, it is to consciousness you must turn, for it is the only foundation on which the phenomena of life can be explained. If we accept the idea of a first cause, it would follow that the evolution of that cause could never result in anything foreign to itself.

That is, if the first cause-substance is light, all its evolutions, fruits and manifestations would remain light. The first cause-substance being consciousness, all its evolutions, fruits and phenomena must remain consciousness. All that could be observed would be a higher or lower form or variation of the same thing. In other words, if your consciousness is the only reality, it must also be the only substance. Consequently, what appears to you as circumstances, conditions and even material objects is really only the product of your own consciousness. Nature, then, as a thing or a complex of things external to your mind, must be rejected. You and your environment cannot be regarded as existing separately. You and your world are one.

**Your "I AMness" is God.** God is everywhere and in all things. There is nothing outside yourself. You are the center of all creation and all revolves around you. As long as we believe in travel, time and disease, we must experience them. In other words, we must have proof of our convictions.

**When we act from the standpoint of body** or personality, we separate life from living, Spirit from matter. We cannot hope to claim our Good, for we are reversing the process. If God is all, there cannot be God and something else. There can be no shadows without light. There can be no outside without an inside. There can be no Jesus without a Christ. There can be no effect without a cause. It is done unto you as you believe. We limit the expression of the I AM through our belief in limitation. The Divine Law will produce anything we choose. It will produce prosperity instead of poverty, health instead of sickness.

The Law is, but It must be definitely specialized. Until we specialize It, It is only a latent possibility. Through this Law, we set the Principle in which we live in motion. When we do not use the Law consciously and constructively, we are using It unconsciously and, it may be, destructively. Prayer is the mental act through which we specialize the Law for specific purposes. In the Silence, we are responsive to the Law. Silence is the home of the soul. It is always at rest, always at peace, always in repose.

**You must turn from the objective appearance** of things to the subjective center of things, your consciousness (your I AMness), if you truly desire to know the cause of the phenomena of life, and how to use this knowledge to realize your fondest dreams. In the midst of the apparent contradictions, antagonisms and contrasts of your life, there is only one principle at work, only your consciousness operating. Difference does not consist in variety of substance, but in variety of arrangement of the same cause-substance, your consciousness.

The world moves with motiveless necessity. By this is meant that it has no motive of its own, but is under the necessity of manifesting your concept, the arrangement of your mind, and your mind is always arranged in the image of all you believe and consent to as true. The rich man, poor man, beggar man or thief are not different minds, but different arrangements of the same mind, in the same sense that a piece of steel, when magnetized, differs not in substance from its demagnetized state, but in the arrangement and order of its molecules.

**It is impossible to conceive of anything other** than the Word of God being that which sets power in motion. God speaks and it is done! It is evident that First Cause must be Self-Existent, i.e., It must be Causeless. Nothing could come before That Which was First. Hence the Being Whom we call GOD must be Self-Existent. God speaks and it is done. If God speaks, His Word must be Law. The Word of God is also the Law of God. God is Word, God is Law, God is Spirit. This is self-evident. We arrive at the conclusion that God as Spirit is Conscious Life. This is the inner meaning of the teaching of the "I AM."

**Man's chief delusion is his conviction** that there are causes other than his own state of (I AMness) consciousness. All that befalls a man . . all that is done by him, all that comes from him . . happens as a result of his state of (I AMness) consciousness. A man's consciousness is all that he thinks and desires and loves, all that he believes is true and consents to. That is why a change of consciousness is necessary before you can change your outer world. Rain falls as a result of a change in the temperature in the higher regions of the atmosphere, so, in like manner, a change of circumstance happens as a result of a change in your state of consciousness. "Be ye transformed by the renewing of your mind." To be transformed, the whole basis of your thoughts must change. But your thoughts cannot change unless you have new ideas, for you think from your ideas. All transformation begins with an intense, burning desire to be transformed.

The first step in the "renewing of the mind" is desire. You must want to be different [and intend to be] before you can begin to change yourself. Then you must make your future dream a present fact. You do this by assuming the feeling of your wish fulfilled (I AM That). By desiring to be other than what you are, you can create an ideal of the person you want to be and assume that you are already that person. If this assumption is persisted in until it becomes your dominant feeling, the attainment of your ideal is inevitable. The ideal you hope to achieve is always ready for an incarnation, but unless you yourself offer it human parentage, it is incapable of birth. Therefore, your attitude should be one in which having desired to express a higher state – you alone accept the task of incarnating this new and greater value of yourself.

**As the iron worker pours the molten iron** into his sand mold, he knows that it will take the shape of the mold. You must be just as meticulous as he in preparing the mold that you wish Creative Principle to fill and just as certain of the result. The visualizing and imaging faculties are the transcendent powers that cause the living Substance of God to flow freely, but It will fill only those molds prepared for it. As you mentally hold your picture in the dark room of the Silence, vigilantly guard against the intrusion of any vagrant thoughts that may distort your image. As your picture is impressed upon your consciousness, it becomes the center of attraction, and the I AM fills it with Substance. It becomes the property of the Universal Mind.

At this point of development, Spirit specializes and differentiates your desire. The power which projects the originating Substance out from Itself is your I AM, and this Substance takes the specific shape which you have given it in your mind. The Universal becomes particular as you recognize that your mind is the particular center through which your I AM is seeking expression in a material sense.

**The highest mental practice is to listen** to this Inner Voice and to declare Its Presence. The greater a man's consciousness of this Indwelling I AM, the more fully he will live. This will never lead to illusion, but will always lead to Reality. All great souls have known this and have constantly striven to let the Mind of God express through their mentalities. "The Father that dwelleth in me, He doeth the works." This was the declaration of the great Master, and it should be ours also; not a limited sense of life but a limitless one.

**Withdraw into the closet of mind. Shut the doors of sight,** sound, touch, taste, smell. When you enter this closet, when you get in there, know this . . "I AM." Think about yourself something like this . . I AM a three-fold being. In my nature I AM physical and I AM spiritual. And all through my spiritual and my physical natures I have mind. In my mind are two things, consciousness and a Force. I AM . . I AM . . I AM made in the image and likeness of my Father, the Great Universal Father who is Universal Spirit, substance and Mind. He is Universal Mind which is filled with Universal Consciousness. His Universal Spirit pervades His mind and substance and is the Force which is all love, all life, all intelligence. He supplies me with His infinite, limitless force, which reinforces and multiplies the force already within me so that I can keep drawing upon the supply as long as I keep giving out. I AM . . I AM . . I AM one with the Father. I AM . . I AM . . I AM divine creator. I AM. I create with the force of God.

**God (I AM, consciousness) is the giver and the gift; man is the receiver.** God (I AM, consciousness) dwells in man, and this means that the treasure house of infinite riches is within you and all around you. By learning the laws of mind, you can extract from that infinite storehouse within you everything you need in order to live life gloriously, joyously, and abundantly.

**The I AM cannot live consciously without giving** expression to life; and the giving of expression to life demands an instrument through which that expression can take place. If there were no manifestation the I AM would simply exist in a state of unconscious abstraction, and we can conceive of no reason why the I AM should exist at all if its existence simply meant eternal sleep in the absolute.

We must have a reason for things; things must explain their existence or state of being in a satisfactory manner; and if anything exists at all there must be some cause for that existence. However, we can find no cause for an existence that would mean nothing more than isolation in an abstract state, or eternal sleep. We must accept, therefore, the other view, or rather the higher understanding of this great theme.

**When you have completely given the body** over to God and it is free, easy and silent, you are ready to step into that new dimension of mind . . the Silence. You are entering the divine Presence of the I AM. You are approaching the state of consciousness that unifies with Intelligence, Power, Substance, Wisdom, Life and Love. Your vision and thought must be single to the I AM in the realization that there is nothing but God.

By staying the mind upon your own I AM, you absorb something of the spiritual environment which you have entered. Your nature takes on the Divine Nature. The beginner in this work will find that the door to the closet will fly open many times during this period and that many unwelcome thoughts will knock. Do not arouse yourself to resist them. Dismiss them by saying something like this, "Go away now. This is not your time or place. If you are important, I'll think about you later."

**The Spirit being all there is, we cannot conceive** of anything that can hinder its working. When the Spirit has spoken, the Word becomes Law, for before the Law is the Word; It precedes all else. First is Absolute Intelligence, All-Power, All-Presence, All-Causation; then the movement upon itself through the power of the Word; then the Word becoming Law; the Law producing the thing and holding it in place. So long as the Word exists the thing will exist, for since the Word is All-Power there is nothing beside It. "I AM That I AM, and beside me there is none other." This "I AM" is Spirit, God, All.

There is no physical explanation for anything in the universe; all causation is Spirit and all effect spiritual. We are not living in a physical world but in a spiritual world peopled with spiritual ideas. We are now living in Spirit. God, or Spirit, governs the universe through great mental laws that work out the divine will and purpose, always operating from Intelligence. This Intelligence is so vast, and the power so great that our human minds cannot even grasp it; all that we can hope to do is to learn something of the way in which it works, and by harmonizing ourselves with it, to so align ourselves with Spirit that our lives may be controlled by the great harmony that obtains in all the higher laws of nature, but has been very imperfectly manifested in man.

I **alone possess the power of the first person**. I AM That which I want to be. Except I believe I AM what I want to be, I remain as I formerly was and die in that limitation.

## Here is a method by which you may have constant contact with Universal Mind.

The method is called the "Silence." It is a mistake to think that the Silence is a state of passivity only. It may be that, to be sure, but for the most practical results it is a work shop. It is where we realize our contact with the great Power and certainly this Universal Power or Mind is ever active, omnipresent, eternal Energy. The Silence as understood by many is subjective and negative. It is subjective, to be sure, but positive. In our present understanding, the subjective side of life is positive and if there is any negative side it is the objective.

It is the within" of all things that is dynamic. The germ within the kernel of wheat, within the tulip bulb, within the acorn or the egg is the creative side of the expression. The shell or husk is important, but always remember that the wheat, flower, tree and chick come from the dynamic center.

Remember, the negative electrons revolve around the positive proton at the center of the group. This point in man is the solar plexus and all his objective activities evolve from that center. The Universal Mind or God flows into man's body through the soles of his feet, through the tips of his fingers and through his head. Just as the sun's rays may be focused at the very center of a magnifying glass, so I AM "in the midst of thee" is mighty.

I AM is localized in you as a point within a circle. The circle could not be drawn without some point as a center; so your outer (objective) life could not exist (stand forth) without this I AM center within you. Man, like the prodigal son, has gone into the far country (surface . . objective, sense life) and has met or rather created difficulties for himself. His only salvation is to return to his home (center . . God . . "I AM").

When he does he will find music, dancing, joy, food, and abundance of all good things. Man must come back consciously to the God within him. This is done by the method of the Silence. "Be still [objectively-physically] and know that "I AM" . . God." One moment spent in quiet meditation (where real thinking takes place) upon the subjective side (God's side), will make all our struggles, doubts, false pride and fears sink into utter nothingness. We realize our Oneness with God by realizing in the Silence that God alone thinks and works. When we are conscious that our thought is really not our thought but God's thought through us, we shall be prosperous and happy. You see, when the realization of the "I AM" is attained, you will be conscious of thinking and speaking from the center of your Being.

There are many books relative to the benefits to be derived from going into the Silence. The great need is to know how to enter it, for when this secret has once been learned, the advantages which come to the seeker are self-evident. The following rules are given to guide you into the way of Truth:

I. SILENCE FOR RELAXATION Practice this Silence at night before going to sleep. Through the application of these suggestions I have known all forms of nervousness to disappear in a week:

1. Lie flat (no pillow) in bed.

2. Extend arms side horizontally: palms up; fingers bent slightly upward.

3. Close eyes.

4. Let go. Let all the weight of your body rest on the bed.

5. Rest for a moment.

6. Repeat each of the following statements seven or eight times, slowly and restfully:

A. I rest in the sea of Universal Energy.

B. This Energy is Good.

C. I AM one with It.

D. I AM IT.

This will take about ten minutes. Do not move a muscle of your body during the Silence, for you are relaxing. If you find some difficulty at first in being quiet, you might say, "Peace be still," for five minutes.

If you go to sleep in this position, perfectly relaxed, you will derive much benefit therefrom. After having this Silence, you may make an audible request such as any of the following: "I want to be guided to an individual who wishes to employ me"; "I want to have the companionship of someone whose thoughts are harmonious with mine"; "I want to attract a buyer for my home"; "I want to make the right move in business"; "I want to know how to improve my health." You see you first make your conscious contact with Universal Mind by going over the statements given. Then you commit to Universal Mind your desire and your subconscious mind which never sleeps, will work faithfully while your objective mind is shut off in sleep. "Let" Universal Mind work; remember you do not make it work; you step out of the way.

## II. SILENCE FOR THE REALIZATION OF "I AM"

1. This Silence will be practiced while the student sits in a chair.

   A. Always select the same chair.

   B. Always have a straight-backed chair.

   C. Have the same time for your Silence each day.

   D. Always have the chair in the same room and in the same place. The reason for this is that you enter the vibrations of the former day, by going where those vibrations are.

THE SUGGESTIONS GIVEN ABOVE ARE VERY IMPORTANT.

   E. The student will sit erect and close the eyes. A straight spine aids concentration.

   F. Place both feet flat on the floor.

   G. Have the head well poised.

   H. Allow both hands to rest either on your knees or in your lap. See that they are relaxed.

   I. You must not move from this position for one-half hour.

2. Affirm quietly each of the following, seven times:

   A. I AM receptive to Universal Good.

   B. I do not resist.

   C. I let go.

3. The next statement should be spoken once. You must be positive in speaking it, because you are going to shut out all thoughts except those which you wish to think. You can "close the door of your mind" by practice. See to this, for it is very important. Affirm . . "I close the door."

4. The next step is just as important. Now that the door is closed, your stream of thought activity cannot go out into the world. It must be directed in and down. Do not try to think thoughts at this point. Your mental stream is like a flowing river. Just direct the stream in and down.

5. As you feel the stream of mental activity flowing in, you will aid your realization by saying quietly, "Down . . Down . . Down" . . three times. As you say it, just imagine that you are in an elevator, going down into a mine. As you descend, the noise of the world grows very dim, until you enter the deepest part of yourself. While you are going down into the "secret place," you will remember many things which you thought you had forgotten. This takes place as you go through the subconscious.

6. When you have reached the center (solar plexus), begin to assert the "I"

7. Repeat the following (each seven times):

a. "I."

b. "I AM."

c. "I AM" . . (always a slight pause after the phrase "I AM") Perfect.

d. "I AM" . . Perfect Life.

e. "I AM" . . Perfect Health.

f. "I AM" . . Happiness.

g. "I AM" . . Success.

All this time you are thinking and speaking from the center.

8. You may now go forth in the "I AM" consciousness. You can reasonably expect a remarkable change to become manifest in your physical, mental and financial affairs.

Do not allow these rules to worry you. Follow the spirit of them and do it easily.

## SUMMARY

1. Gain "Understanding" through reading these lessons.

2. Be faithful with your "Silence."

3. Realize God ("I AM") and you will always desire the right thing.

4. Follow these four rules:

a. Know what you want.

b. State what you want. State it audibly once in a definite tone of understanding faith, before the "Silence."

c. Have your Silence for the realization of the "I AM."

d. State that you have your desire in substance, after the silence.

**The Great Affirmation, therefore,** is the perception that the "I AM" is ONE, always harmonious with itself, and including all things in this harmony for the simple reason that there is no second creative power; and when the individual realizes that this always-single power is the root of his own being, and therefore has center in himself and finds expression through him, he learns to trust its singleness and the consequent harmony of its action in him with what it is doing around him. Then he sees that the affirmation "I and my Father are ONE" is a necessary deduction from a correct apprehension of the fundamental principles of being; and then, on the principle that the less must be included in the greater, he desires that harmonious unity of action be maintained by the adaptation of his own particular movement to the larger movement of the Spirit working as the Creative Principle through the great whole. In this way we become centers through which the creative forces find specialization by the development of that personal factor on which the specific application of general laws must always depend.

**The truth is that if we are just as necessary** to God as God is to us, we have therein the real principle and the real need of divine unity. We all must admit that it is inconceivable to think of the family of human souls as being one with God if neither were necessary to the other; but the fact that they are all necessary to each other gives an eternal reason for endless unity between the Infinite and every soul in existence. The same idea is applicable to the individual I AM and the manifested life of the personality. Our conclusion here must be that although the individual I AM is perfect in being, living in the absolute, still manifestation through the personality is absolutely necessary to the conscious existence of the I AM.

**"The word is creative,"** as **Emmet Fox says,** "and the strongest and most creative word is "I AM." Whenever you say "I AM," you are calling upon the Universe to do something for you, and it will do it. Whenever you say "I AM," you are drawing a check upon the Universe. It will be honored and cashed sooner or later, and the proceeds will go to you. If you say 'I AM tired, sick, poor, fed up, disappointed, getting old,' then you are drawing checks for future trouble and limitation. When you say, 'I AM divine Life, I AM divine Truth, I AM divine Freedom, I AM divine Substance, I AM eternal Substance,' you are drawing a check on the bank of Heaven, and surely that check will be honored with health and plenty for you. "Remember you don't have to use the actual grammatical form, 'I AM.' Every time you associate yourself in thought with anything or think of yourself as having anything, you are using a form of 'I AM.' The verb to have is a part of the verb to be. In the very ancient languages there is no verb to have. It is a modern improvement, like the radio or the automobile. I have means I AM because you always have what you are and you always do what you are."

**When Jesus said, "No man cometh unto the Father** but by me," of course, he meant the I AM. This I AM, then, means the inner Reality of every man's nature, and when we stop to figure it out, how can we come unto God, the Living Spirit, except through the avenues of our own consciousness, which is the only approach to God we could possibly have? It is another way of saying that the only way we shall ever approach Reality is by uncovering the Divinity already latent within our own consciousness, in our own soul, in the center of our own being.

## The Inner Force of Thought

**There are certain forms of mental action** that exercise a direct power upon the human personality, while there are other forms of mental action that do not exercise that power. How to tell the difference between the two is a great problem, and a most important problem, because to find the solution is to find the real secret of practical results in the metaphysical field. Those who have tried to secure results through the application of right thinking have found that at times results came almost instantaneously, while at other times it seemed almost impossible to accomplish anything, even though the same methods were employed to the letter. Then there are many who never secure any results whatever, though they apply the same principle, as those who are exceptionally successful, and the reason why seems a mystery. The mystery disappears, however, when we learn that thought does not become power unless the inner force of thought is brought into action.

Two persons may with the same enthusiasm and perseverance affirm "I AM well"; one finds no change, while the other begins to mend at once, and is soon restored to perfect health. The same idea and the same method was employed in each case, but only in the one did thought become power. In like manner two persons of equal intelligence may live according to the same system of metaphysics or idealism. The one gains ground every day, while the other finds conditions no better than he did while employing his previous helter-skelter modes of thought. It is evident, therefore, that it is not the thought itself that produces results, but some power that is back of or within thought.

**As it takes faith to leave the old state** of material bondage wherein we receive only that which the law of sense determines for us, and again an increase of faith to meet the tests that compel us to rely upon the unseen power to provide for the daily needs, still again it requires faith in an intensified degree to know I AM supply, . . that where I AM God is, and where God is, all is. Therefore, abundance is here where I AM, for I AM the boundless, limitless abundance of power, substance and intelligence of God, present in all places, under all circumstances and at all times. This is the promised land, the fulfillment of faith that admits of no limitation, that recognizes no lack, that abides in the consciousness of abundance and hence lives and loves and gives. It is the exercising of faith that "worketh by love," for love is the fulfilling of the law, . . the perfecting of it.

**Creation is finished and perfect.** There is actually nothing to heal or be added from the outside. God is that which I AM; my purpose is not to demonstrate things, but to reveal, or to give out from my Center, what that Center is. I can do that only by keeping myself in absolute harmony with that which I AM. Acknowledge him in all the ways. I AM saved from all untoward circumstances only by virtue of what I AM, by the Life Principle of the Universal Mind. I AM the way, the truth and the life. My mission is to cooperate with the Universal Consciousness in my own mind. The circumstances of my life will automatically express the harmonious action of my thought.

## SELF-AWARENESS

**Often when I am teaching classes** I have the students take
the two words, I AM, and put their full attention on just
these two words for thirty seconds, or perhaps a full minute.
I ask them not to relate these words to body or profession, or
to the immediate situation. They are to think exclusively I
AM and nothing more. Try it in the quiet of your own home.
As I often say, that which I AM is not name and number. It is
unconditioned and free. That is what you are contemplating.
You are contemplating the essence of being, and that is what
the great spiritual thinkers, both East and West, did. These
great minds have taken a moment, or a few moments, on a
disciplined basis, to deal with that which they were which
was not name or profession; which while it used body was
not body; and which, while it used intellect was not intellect.
They were dealing with Pure Cause before it became Effect.
You are always cause becoming effect. That is why your mind
creates out of itself. That is why your emotions create out of
themselves; whether it be a gracious home, a family, or a
great business enterprise. By means of the individual, cause
is always becoming effect.

**The real man is the soul** or the individuality the "I AM"; and
that part of man is always perfectly well; in fact, cannot
possibly be otherwise than well, a statement that can be
demonstrated to the scientifically exact. To know that this is
true, and to know that you yourself are the real man that
something in human nature that is always perfectly well, is
to know the truth the truth that makes man free.

**When man discovers his I AM** to be the impersonal power
of expression, which power eternally personifies itself in his
conceptions of himself, he will assume and appropriate that
state of consciousness which he desires to express; in so
doing he will become that state in expression. "Ye shall
decree a thing and it shall come to pass" can now be told in
this manner: You shall become conscious of being or
possessing a thing and you shall express or possess that
which you are conscious of being. The law of consciousness
is the only law of expression. "I AM the way". "I AM the
resurrection".

**I AM is the Super Mind, the sum** total of God-
Consciousness; the action of this mind is always within and
upon Itself. It is the complement of the other two minds and
the container of both. The three in reality are one. There is
only one mind, the Universal Mind of God. Mind and
Consciousness are interchangeable terms. Conscious and
subconscious are two names for the One Mind.
Subconscious and subjective mean the same thing . . the
mind and the law of the soul. Unlimited power is available to
man as he consciously uses the creative force. The I AM
which we discover in our own consciousness is the Principle
we use in our work in the Silence. Both conscious and
subjective minds are the instruments of the I AM.

## THE LAW OF CREATION

**Let us take one of the stories of the Bible and see how the prophets and writers of old revealed the story of creation by this strange Eastern symbolism.**

We all know the story of Noah and the Ark; that Noah was chosen to create a new world after the world was destroyed by the flood.

The Bible tells us that Noah had three sons, Shem, Ham and Japheth.

The first son is called Shem, which means name. Ham, the second son, means warm, alive. The third son is called Japheth, which means extension. You will observe that Noah and his three sons Shem, Ham and Japheth contain the same formula of creation as does the divine name of JOD HE VAU HE.

Noah, the Father, the conceiver, the builder of a new world is equivalent to the JOD, or unconditioned consciousness, I AM. Shem is your desire; that which you are conscious of; that which you name and define as your objective, and is equivalent to the second letter in the divine name (HE). Ham is the warm, live state of feeling, which joins or binds together consciousness desiring and the thing desired, and is therefore equivalent to the third letter in the divine name, the VAU. The last son, Japheth, means extension, and is the extended or objectified state bearing witness of the subjective state and is equivalent to the last letter in the divine name, HE.

You are Noah, the knower, the creator. The first thing you beget is an idea, an urge, a desire, the word, or your first son Shem (name).

Your second son Ham (warm, alive) is the secret of FEELING by which you are joined to your desire subjectively so that you, the consciousness desiring, become conscious of being or possessing the thing desired.

Your third son, Japheth, is the confirmation, the visible proof that you know the secret of creation. He is the extended or objectified state bearing witness of the invisible or subjective state in which you abide.

In the story of Noah it is recorded that Ham saw the secrets of his Father, and, because of his discovery, he was made to serve his brothers, Shem and Japheth. Ham, or feeling, is the secret of the Father, your I AM, for it is through feeling that the consciousness desiring is joined to the thing desired.

The conscious union or mystical marriage is made possible only through feeling. It is feeling which performs this heavenly union of Father and Son, Noah and Shem, unconditioned consciousness and conditioned consciousness.

By performing this service, feeling automatically serves Japheth, the extended or expressed state, for there can be no objectified expression unless there is first a subjective impression.

To feel the presence of the thing desired, to subjectively actualize a state by impressing upon yourself, through feeling, a definite conscious state is the secret of creation.

Your present objectified world is Japheth which was made visible by Ham. Therefore Ham serves his brothers Shem and Japheth, for without feeling which is symbolized as Ham, the idea or thing desired (Shem) could not be made visible as Japheth.

The ability to feel the unseen, the ability to actualize and make real a definite subjective state through the sense of feeling is the secret of creation, the secret by which the word or unseen desire is made visible – is made flesh. "And God calleth things that be not as though they were".

Consciousness calls things that are not seen as though they were, and it does this by first defining itself as that which it desires to express, and second by remaining within the defined state until the invisible becomes visible.

Here is the perfect working of the law according to the story of Noah. This very moment you are aware of being. This awareness of being, this knowing that you are, is Noah, the creator.

Now with Noah's identity established as your own consciousness of being, name something that you would like to possess or express; define some objective (Shem), and with your desire clearly defined, close your eyes and feel that you have it or are expressing it.

Don't question how it can be done; simply feel that you have it. Assume the attitude of mind that would be yours if you were already in possession of it so that you feel that it is done.

Feeling is the secret of creation.

Be as wise as Ham and make this discovery that you too may have the joy of serving your brothers Shem and Japheth; the joy of making the word or name flesh.

**When we look into the creative way of the spirit** we find it impossible for denial to enter, as the Spirit recognizes no opposite to its own nature. It knows that "I AM and beside me there is no other." The Spirit does not deny anything, it simply affirms itself to be that which it desires to be. Seeing and recognizing no opposite to itself, it finds no need of denial, indeed, this thought need not enter the mind; if we are working with the Spirit we need not deny but state the affirmative attitude of mind, realizing that we are dealing with the only power that exists.

There is a subtle danger in using denials; we may deny to such an extent as to erect a barrier or build a mountain to overcome. Once realize that God makes things out of Himself simply by speaking, and you will never again use denials in treating. All that needs changing is the false thought, and by affirming that your word destroys everything but itself you will embody all that a denial could. In those systems that teach denials we find that the more enlightened ones are gradually using the affirmative method, and as this is the growth of experience there can be no doubt that it is the better method. Of one thing we may be sure, the Spirit never denies. It simply knows that I AM.

**Why is it possible for one person to do** what another person cannot do? Because the one realizes and recognizes it possible and the other does not. When you realize that there is only one Consciousness, one Intelligence, one Substance (God Infinite), and that you are an expression of God Infinite, you can say: "I and the Father are one" . . in body, in mind, in spirit. But when you accept separation, you usurp the authority of the great "I AM" . . God. When you usurp that authority you begin thinking imperfectly, and, by that same "I AM" within you, you bring forth that which is not perfect. How is it possible to bring forth that which is perfect?

Allow God, with His Perfect Intelligence, to work through you. The simplicity of it is so great that it overwhelms us. Aspiration is the method you must use to begin with, then you become filled with Divine Love, Wisdom and Power which act together in perfect harmony, and growth becomes as natural as that of the flowers.

**We must first be before we can do,** and we can do only to the extent to which we are. We cannot express powers which we do not possess; so that our doing necessarily coincides with the quality of our being. Therefore the Divine Verb reproduces the Divine Substantive by a natural sequence. It is generated by the Divine "I AM," and for this reason it is called "The Son of God." So we see that The Verb, The Word, and The Son of God, are all different expressions for the same Power.

**The formation or wording of an affirmation** should be left to the individual, and in each instance that affirmation should give expression to the highest conception of truth that has been attained. An affirmation should not deal with relative truth, but with absolute truth; and the difference can be illustrated by the two statements, "I AM better," and "I AM well." The statement, "I AM better," is a relative truth, it deals with a changing state and no changing state can serve as a permanent ideal for right thinking. Therefore, such affirmations are of very little value.

The statement, "I AM well," is an absolute truth, because in the absolute or in the perfect all is well; and we can conceive of no higher ideal in the world of wholeness than that of being absolutely well. Such a statement therefore gives expression to the real truth as it is, and will also inspire the mind to produce thought and mental states in the exact likeness of that truth.

**When the man outside merges with the Man Inside,** he knows himself to be not only the prayer but the answer also. As man feels this Divinity stirring and as It reaches forth to control his subjective life, Silence will become a part of his everyday living. But it must not become merely a means of receiving loaves and fishes. The I AM is indifferent to things because it recognizes nothing apart from Itself. It desires only man's unity with Itself. In this unity man embodies his Good. In the intangible world of Spirit, all things needful to man are classified under the heading of Good. If we seek the supremacy of Good (God), we shall never lack. Not until we withdraw our thought from the relative plane are we able to cultivate our inner resources.

**This room is not filled with air. It is filled with that thinking Substance** and as you think into it and speak into it, it vibrates. As you cause it to vibrate, you bring it into form. No one else in the universe is responsible for my good or evil but myself, and instead of blaming fate for conditions, I should "treat" myself and analyze my consciousness. Then I shall discover that I have been thinking and speaking the thing which I have not desired in form. Every thought that goes from your brain is a vibration and brings its results negatively or positively. You cannot say one word without having it register in this universal thinking Substance which we call Mind.

The great Teacher said, "Man shall give an account for every idle word that he speaks." Your day of judgment is now, and at this very time you may be having to face your own thoughts in the form of flesh and blood. "The word became flesh." I can speak my body into a state of health, power or any other condition . . either negative or positive.

"In the beginning was the Word and the Word was with God and the Word was God." As you go to the office with thoughts of financial depression, you are vibrating this wonderful universal thinking Substance . . Mind . . and you are causing it to take negative forms. I cannot think without having the results of that thought. It is always cause and effect. "It has become apparent that however different one phenomenon is from another, the factors of both are the same, so that all the so-called forces of nature considered as objective things are reduced to nothing more mysterious than push and pull" . . a state of vibration. The things which we see are vibrating at the lowest rate and those which we cannot see are in the highest vibration.

The man or woman who lives in a high state of consciousness or high state of vibration is the one who is not so conscious of things. The people who have an unusual degree of wisdom are those who have learned to think in the higher realms of consciousness, and who have been in touch with these higher vibrations.

"**The universe has a center which is its Source,** and it has a periphery which is that part of itself farthest away from the Source, and in general it is shaped like a sphere, but its structure follows the plan of the pyramid. At the tip of the pyramid is the Source . . the Ultimate Being . . the I AM consciousness referred to as God. The Source at rest is in a condition of perfect balance and is all light, all power, and all truth, but in order to better understand itself it deliberately produces in itself a condition of imbalance and thus becomes creative, descending from its absolute state and dividing into two opposing but complementary forces . . Space and Time. Imbalanced, they descend into matter. Balanced, they ascend into Spirit.

"**Except ye believe not that I AM he,** ye shall die in your sins." Do you know that no two in this room live in the same world. We are going home to different worlds tonight. We close our doors on entirely different worlds. We rise tomorrow and go to work, where we meet each other and meet others, but we live in different mental worlds, different physical worlds. I can only give what I AM, I have no other gift to give. If I want the world to be perfect, and who does not, I have failed only because I did not know that I could never see it perfect until I myself become perfect. If I AM not perfect I cannot see perfection, but the day that I become it, I beautify my world because I see it through my own eyes. "Unto the pure all things are pure."

**To reach the spiritual consciousness all mankind** is
striving for today, we must be ever conscious of the Divine
Law of God; and to live that Law, we must be conscious of
and know: I AM Immortal. I AM Invincible. I AM Power. I AM
Mind. I AM Soul I AM Intelligence. I AM Life. I AM God.

Now meditate and think of what you have said, until you are
conscious of what it really means. For example:

I AM Immortal: the God within me is Immortal,
unchangeable and cannot be destroyed.

I AM Invincible: the God within me Is invincible, insuperable,
unconquerable.

I AM Power: all things are possible for me if I know how to
use my mind . . the God-power within me . . constructively;
and think only good, love, happiness and prosperity.

By using my mind correctly, I AM a creator . . the creator of
my universe in which I live, peopled by my thoughts, deeds
and actions.

I AM Soul: Soul is Spirit manifested. Soul is Mother-God,
Mother-nature, Mother-earth. Soul is all the Life, all the
Power, all the Love, all the substance and intelligence in the
Universe manifested.

I AM Intelligence: I am using all the intelligence in the
universe if I am expressing the I AM, or God, within . .
through love for all humanity, regardless of creed, color or
nationality.

I AM Life: I AM the reflection of God. My physical body is my
reflection . . my proof of how much of God I am expressing. It

is the instrument through which God is expressing His
Power and Life. It is my tangible proof of God.

I AM God: I AM God as Soul, Mind, Intelligence, Power and
Life.

If you have meditated and thought intelligently of the above,
you cannot possibly doubt
that you . . the I AM . . are God.

"**God is Substance, God is my supply.** His Substance now,
through definite Law, is the supply of my experience. Every
good thing comes to me, and only good goes out from me."
Suppose we do that and it does not work. Just remember
this: Act as though I AM, and I will be." That is one of the
wisest things ever said. If we try and fail there is nothing to
do but to try again, and perhaps try in a better way.

Perhaps we need to be a little more certain that we are not
limiting the Divine Principle to what we consider as
unchangeable facts.

God makes facts just as fast as God images, pictures, or
contemplates His own Being. So out of our contemplation,
out of our prayer or treatment, shall be established a new
fact which shall correspond and be equivalent to the form of
that idea envisioned in the treatment. Indwelling every soul
there is a Divine Something, call It what you will, that is
creative of our destiny.

## DESIRE, THE WORD OF GOD

**"So shall My word be that goeth forth out of My mouth;** it shall not return unto Me void, but it shall accomplish that which I please, and it shall prosper in the thing whereunto I sent it."

God speaks to you through the medium of your basic desires. Your basic desires are words of promise or prophecies that contain within themselves the plan and power of expression.

By basic desire is meant your real objective. Secondary desires deal with the manner of realization. God, your I AM, speaks to you, the conditioned conscious state, through your basic desires. Secondary desires or ways of expression are the secrets of your I AM, the all wise Father. Your Father, I AM, reveals the first and last . . "I AM the beginning and the end" . . but never does He reveal the middle or secret of His ways; that is, the first is revealed as the word, your basic desire. The last is its fulfillment . . the word made flesh. The second or middle (the plan of unfoldment) is never revealed to man but remains forever the Father's secret.

**While meditating, an effort should always be made** in the I AM consciousness to command the forces of the mind, the emotions, and the physical senses to be still and know that You . . the God of you . . speaks and must be obeyed.

**Symbolically, man's body has been likened** to a triangle, divided horizontally into three parts, or the mystic fusion of the three aspects of his creator, consciousness, vibration and love. At the base of this triangle we have the material, the earthy aspects of life. In the middle we have the mental or intelligence side or aspect of life, and at the apex of the triangle we have the enlightening, the understanding, the illuminating, the conscious, the spiritual aspects of life, crowning the most sublime creature modeled by the intelligence that created all ideals.

Let us realize, therefore, that our life should be organized in all its factors, physical, mental and spiritual. Yes, because I have substance or material within my body temple, I must renew it. I have weight. I have movement. I occupy space. I have mind-stuff or consciousness within my body temple. I can think. I can use my five senses. I can will. I can enjoy. I can reason and realize. And I have Spirit within my body temple. I AM not only the Known, but I AM the Knower of it all.

**If you lack abundance, or some friend is in need,** command the I AM Power within you to bring forth out of the infinite abundance the wherewithal for these needs. If you do this in the right spirit, in the consciousness that God in you is doing the work, and that God expresses only in divine love, harmony, life and abundance, then you will know all the forces of the Universe will work together to the desired end, and in the Father's good time it shall manifest.

**Now I am going to ask you to start building** your basic thought for prosperity without further delay. Center your thought again in our affirmation: I AM PROSPERITY. This is the nucleus that is to grow and multiply indefinitely. It must be backed up with your earnest faith and desire. Your idea of prosperity may be a better position, more income, a nice vacation, an agreeable companion, or more health. It may be something you do not have but need desperately. The Law says that you can have anything you desire if you believe that you already have it; that is, if you have a subjective acceptance of the thing desired.

Now contemplate that for a few moments . . not the money to meet the mortgage, not the new car, not the new house but THE BASIC IDEA: I AM PROSPERITY. You are going to change your Consciousness out of the old mold of lack and into the new mold of plenty. You are going to create a new habit atmosphere and new thought inclinations. That is your big responsibility in the process. You are going to eradicate a mental equivalent of lack by substituting a mental equivalent of plenty. You are going to start this idea of Prosperity revolving on its axis at such a high rate of speed that it will draw into your life all the good things you need.

Now put the book down . . close your eyes . . relax . . and repeat the affirmation slowly and with pointed purpose one hundred times. Take it easy, and feel your pattern deeply. Realize that with each repetition your new idea is going further and further underground until it is perfectly integrated with the Creative Mind. It now has the power to attract to itself all the elements that it needs for its fulfillment. The rest of the process is a matter of sustained attention, faith, feeling, acting, and seeing.

See the new idea clearly. Realize it, feel it, and accept it. Speed it up with your belief. Keep it alive with your faith.

Feed it with fresh, rich, powerful, and life-giving images. Give it motion through action. Act it out. I AM PROSPERITY. Realize how rich you are. Keep the prosperity ideas and thoughts circulating freely through your mind. See them generating abundance, opportunities, and success. Do not allow negative ideas to creep in and short circuit your good. I AM PROSPERITY. Keep repeating it until it goes underground and takes form. I AM PROSPERITY. Feel it. Rejoice in it. Bless it. Love it. Speed up the rate of vibration by telling your subconscious mind that you are already prosperous.

**Harmony is the foundation of your being,** and perfect relaxation enables this harmonious condition to be made manifest. When in this state is the time to repeat your mantra. The saying that Coué invented was: "Day by day, in every respect, I AM getting better and better." Under strict analysis this is not correct, because the I AM and the me are different. The I AM . . GOD . . is the inner Self which is perfect and cannot be made more perfect, but the me is the personal or the outer self, which is affected by our actions and thoughts. Therefore I have altered the saying to: "Day by day, in every way, God is making me better and better." This does not conflict with the truth.

By this method we open ourselves to the inflow of the great Life Principle, the Intelligence. We are benefited, cured of our troubles. If we fear it or do not trust it, we shut the door and we suffer. We must let go of our adverse thoughts, or we prevent the Divine Principle from working through us; for it is the uninterrupted flow of Life within which changes the tissue structure to a healthy condition and eliminates disease.

**"And God said unto Moses, I AM That I AM:** and he said, Thus shalt thou say unto the children of Israel, I AM hath sent me unto you. . . . "This is my name forever, and this is my memorial unto all generations." I AM, then, is God's name. Every time you say I AM sick, I AM weak, I AM discouraged, are you not speaking God's name in vain, falsely? I AM cannot be sick; I AM cannot be weary, or faint, or powerless; for I AM is All Life, All-Power, All-Good. "I AM," spoken with a downward tendency, is always false, always "in vain."

The seventh commandment says, "Take not the name of the Lord thy God in vain; for the Lord will not hold him guiltless that taketh His name in vain." And Jesus said, "By thy words thou shall be justified, and by thy words thou shalt be condemned."

If you speak the "I AM" falsely, you will get the result of false speaking. If you say, "I AM sick," you will get sickness; "I AM poor," you will get poverty; for the law is, "Whatsoever a man soweth, that shall he also reap."

"I AM," spoken upward, toward the good, the true, is sure to out picture in visible good, in success, in happiness. Does all this sound foolish to you? Do you doubt that such power goes with the speaking of that name? If so, just go alone, close your eyes, and in the depth of your own soul say over and over the words, "I AM." Soon you will find your whole being filled with a sense of power which you never had before . . power to overcome, power to accomplish, power to do all things.

**Following is a brief discussion of the phases of consciousness:**

1. The three planes of consciousness and the Self.

Outline:

Conscious Mind

Subjective Mind

Subconscious Mind

"I AM" . . Self

First there is the conscious mind; then the subjective mind; then the subconscious mind and finally the Self or "I AM." The first is the ordinary consciousness or objective mind which we use day by day; that part of Mind of which we are cognizant; with which we commonly think; which we use and are conscious of using in ordinary states.

The subjective mind is the twilight zone between the objective and the subconscious. It is this state of consciousness in which the individual functions when he is neither awake nor asleep. People live in this consciousness too much; they are not thinking from the deeper part of Mind . . neither do they seem to use even the objective or reasoning mind. They are said to be "asleep."

Although they are both open to suggestion, one great difference between the subjective mind and the subconscious mind is to be noted, namely, the subconscious mind creates and objectifies all that it believes; the subjective mind does not. Since the subconscious is the creative mind it begins to work out forms in the visible world, according to the patterns given it by the Self. If the subconscious mind received all the impressions of the objective mind and created them, what a confusion we would have! If all the false beliefs regarding sickness, and all the false ideas of lack were to be received in the subconscious mind, man would live in constant poverty while here and pass on not having learned the Truth.

If you will look at the outline previously given, you will understand the point which I now present. The subjective mind acts as an insulation, keeping out false ideas and thoughts of error from the subconscious . . with this exception, however . . if there is great fear or fright the suggestion goes through and registers in the subconscious. To make this plain let me give you an illustration. If a block of metal were charged with positive electricity and were placed on a similar block charged with negative electricity, the negative block would be charged. However, if there were a sheet of rubber between these blocks, acting as an insulator, it would not receive the current, unless the positive block were highly charged.

People do not really desire things enough or their positive suggestions would come through the subconscious where they would register and bring forth results. Mind in all its activities is the instrument of the Self. In the outline the short line under the subconscious mind represents the real Self . . the "I AM." Man is therefore a threefold being. He is body, Soul and Spirit. "I AM" is Spirit; Soul is Mind (subconscious, subjective and conscious) and body is the visible manifestation of Self produced by Mind. The proper way of thinking and speaking is from the "I AM" consciousness or from the center to the surface; from reality to appearance; from cause to effect. When one says "I AM . . perfect," or "I AM . . success," with the understanding which he gains in the Silence, he demonstrates in the world of visibility.

**The wider the generalization we thus make**, the less we shall need to trouble about particulars, knowing that they will form themselves by the natural action of the Law; and the widest generalization is therefore, to state not what we want to have, but what we want to be. The only reason we ever want to have anything, is because we think it will help us to be something . . something more than we are now; so that the "having" is only a link in the chain of secondary causes, and may therefore be left out of consideration, for it will come of itself through the natural workings of the Law, set in operation by the Word as First Cause. This principle is set forth in the statement of the Divine Name given to Moses. The Name is simply "I AM" . . it is Being, not having . . the having follows as a natural consequence of the Being; and if it be true that we are made in the likeness and image of God, that is to say on the same Principle, then what is the Law of the Divine nature must be the Law of ours also . . and as we awake to this we become "partakers of the Divine Nature"

**I may not like what I have just heard,** that I must turn to my own consciousness . . I AM . . as to the only reality, the only foundation on which all phenomena can be explained. It was easier living when I could blame another. It was much easier living when I could blame society for my ills, or point a finger across the sea. and blame another nation. It was easier living when I could blame the weather for the way I feel. But to tell me that I AM the cause of all that happens to me that I AM forever molding my world in harmony with my inner nature, that is more than man is willing to accept. If this is true, to whom would I go? If these are the words of eternal life, I must return to them, even though they seem so difficult to digest.

**Man in the past has had a material consciousness** and has failed to arrive at the castle of his dreams because of that. Few have realized this to be the fact, but it remains so. A spiritually minded person is the successful person, but how can one have a spiritual mind with a material consciousness? "The double-minded man is unstable in all his ways; let not that man think that he shall receive anything from the Lord." We cannot have any belief in duality. Either God is Mind and all is Mind or God is matter and all is material. The end of the world, generally expressed, has not been fully comprehended. The scientific meaning of that expression is "the end of your belief in the material world." Emerson was told one day that the world was coming to an end and he calmly replied, "I can get along without it." The end of the world has taken place for you, as you reach the realization that the world is spiritually made of this one Spirit . . Mind . . Substance. Remember, I am not denying forms but I am endeavoring to show you that the Substance of forms, or that which "stands under" the form is Mind. The form which we call the body is not physical or material; it is spiritual. A man can say, "I AM Spirit, because I AM made of this one universal Substance." I do not mean that man is Spirit in a physical body . . that is the old idea . . but I mean that his body is made out of this one Substance, one Spirit . . Substance. His body is this Substance brought into visibility. His Soul is of the same Substance but invisible. To illustrate: ice is $H2O$, but it is in a different degree of manifestation. You must know that matter . . so-called . . is Mind. There is one primary Principle, Mind, Substance, which is universal, and this is the scientific understanding of God. I want to prove to you that there is nothing in the universe but Spirit . . Substance. Remember . . this may be vibrating at a low rate and be visible, or it may be in a very high state of vibration and be invisible, so that ( I AM) God is all there is . . visible and invisible.

**Jesus also said, "Whatsoever ye ask in my name"** . . that is, in the name I AM . . "He will give it you." Whenever you desire . . not supplicate, but desire, speaking the "I AM" upward . . He will give what you ask. Every time you say, "I AM happy," you ask in His name for happiness. Every time you say, "I AM unhappy," you ask in His name for unhappiness. "Hitherto," He said to the disciples, "ye have asked nothing in my name. Ask, and ye shall receive, that your joy may be full." Is not this just the trouble? Hitherto what have we been asking "in His name"? Have we been asking for health or sickness, for happiness or unhappiness, for riches or poverty, by the manner of our speaking the I AM? Have we spoken it upward, toward the good, or downward toward the not good? That which we have been receiving will tell the story. Jesus said if they asked rightly in His name, their "joy would be full." Is your joy full? If not, then give heed to your asking. The disciples healed "in the name of Jesus Christ." In the name of Jesus Christ is in the name of the I AM.

**Even though you are overwhelmed by poverty,** sickness and sorrow, affirm the opposite. Say with all the earnestness you can muster: I AM rich, I AM well, I AM happy. Say it again and again, day after day, though all things conspire to give the lie to your words. If you do this faithfully you will at last enable the Subconscious Mind to make your words come true.

**By your realizing this truth, that all is Life,** and, therefore, good, you are enabled to speak the word that becomes the flesh and blood of a regenerated existence. In other words, you are able by a supreme belief in Being, in the allness of Life, or good, and by this supreme belief identifying yourself with it, to speak for what you want, and to get it too; and that without wronging another, because there is no monopoly in the knowledge of truth; and each mind can make its own opulence apparent in the degree of its power to recognize the truth that all is Life, and, therefore, good; thus casting out every belief in evil; every belief in disease, sin, sorrow and death, and leaving Life only, good only, to fill your entire personality.

And of this everlasting good, or Life, such qualities as are recognized as best and most desirable can be affirmed by the student; and affirmed as being already in possession.

Thus, "I AM healthy, I AM strong; I AM intellectual, I have the power of an infinite understanding, I AM great, I AM beautiful, I AM opulent." Any, or all of these affirmations are in order.

And remember that everything that is, is now; that in infinite Being, in the eternal Life Principle, there is no increase and no decay. All exists, and exists in absolute perfectness at one time equally as much as at any other time; and that that which makes any part of this Life, this perfectness apparent is individual recognition.

Therefore, make all your affirmations in the present time, "I AM That which I desire to be, and I AM it now." The external Principle of Life is best expressed in the simple word "Being," which means yesterday, today and forever; or one eternal now.

All is good, and all good is mine. I have health now, because the power dwells within me to compel the perfect action of every function of my body; and all I need to do is to recognize this truth in order to send the negative forces (weakness, disease, pain, etc.) flying, and to utilize my unlimited power. Why, I tell you that you who read these lines have nothing to fear, for no sickness, no tyranny, no negative conditions, no fetter or slavery of any kind whatever can hold or even detain for one moment the growing soul of man after he has entered the domain of the Law of Attraction . . the Principle of Life, the all-good of limitless Being . . by the knowledge of the fact that he is one with all this infinite power; that he has this infinite power within himself, at his daily and hourly command, to set aside any hindrance in the shape of the negative forces which may rise either within or without him.

And what is required to find this power? A living recognition of it. A firm, unshaken belief that it is within you; that it is your all in all. But this you cannot attain in a day or a week. It only comes with the daily striving after truth; the earnest thought and effort to secure truth; and constant living in, and practice of, the highest truth you know. In this way you gradually draw near to the grand results Mental Science promises and reveals; and every twenty-four hours leaves you in possession of an increased understanding. But the increase may be so small as to be immeasurable from day to day, and only discernible at longer periods of comparison. For so it is that we journey up the heights of understanding; ever enjoying the new manifestations of the eternal revealed to our wondering eyes at each advancing step.

The brain, as the most positive part of the organization, takes the lead; and because I know that this organization is all mind, I AM sure that if thought . . the positive leads, the most negative parts will follow. I AM sure that my thought . . the positive part of the magnet me . . will infuse enough of its intelligence into the less intelligent part to show forth the fact that pain and sickness are not positive forces, having inherent power to conquer me, but are negative, amenable to supreme forces . . love, life, intelligence, faith, justice, courage, health, etc.

### "I AM" is Success.

Success is "I AM."

"I AM" the "I AM."

"I AM" . . Success.

This is the meaning of the fourth line . . "I AM" . . Self. It is the God within who is Success, for "I AM" was the original Idea of God.

With these introductory remarks, I shall begin to show you that if you are going to demonstrate your abundant supply you must have the consciousness of that supply. You have not had the consciousness because you have not had the understanding.

Health, Wealth or Happiness is a matter of consciousness. That which you are conscious of, you are and have. If you know Truth you have Truth; if you are conscious of error you entertain a belief in evil. In the past, the first has been called health, prosperity, happiness . . heaven . . the second has been called disease, death, poverty and discord . . hell. Both states are not places but states of consciousness. It is the "consciousness" of Abundance that man needs in order to attract Abundance unto him.

**Look within yourself for the source of all power.** I AM the great power of God expressing as ME. I AM the great abundance for all my needs and a surplus to spare. That to which I give my attention reveals itself. So give your attention to the things you want! Fill your Scrap Book with pictures of them. Put over and under and around them such affirmations as these:

"I AM is able to do exceeding abundantly above all that we ask or think, according to the Power that worketh in us. I rejoice in the bounty of I AM, constantly manifesting to meet my every need."

"If ye abide in Me and my words abide in you, ye shall ask what ye will and it shall be done unto you. For herein is the Father glorified, that ye bear much fruit." "Your Father knoweth what things ye have need of before you ask Him. Fear not, for it is the (I AM) Father's good pleasure to give you the Kingdom. All that the Father hath is yours, and you are in all ways prospered."

"I will give thee hidden riches of secret places, that thou mayest know that I AM the God (I AM) of Israel. Remember that . . "According to thy faith be it done unto you. "So believe that you RECEIVE! If your beliefs are all for the future, you will get them in the distant future but never NOW. You will never quite catch up with them. "Now is the accepted time. Now is the day of salvation." Realize that all these good things are NOW coming into manifestation in your life. Bless and thank God for them NOW.

**Listen now: While the upper brain is Lord of the body** there is yet a higher, which is Lord of All. The I AM That I AM is positive to the brain as the brain is to the body.

The highest brain is the present consciousness of the I AM. This is just as true in the lower order of life as in man himself; as true in primitive man as in Christ. The I AM That I AM is constantly working upon the highest in the individual, to unfold, to make conscious more of itself, the One, to that individual.

The I AM neither slumbers nor sleeps. It acts with omnipresent power, inexorable power, loving power, upon the brain . . pressing for recognition. This it is to which Jesus referred when he declared, "Behold I (the I AM) stand at the door and knock, and if any man will open unto me I will come unto him and sup with him and he with me."

We are told that the atmosphere presses upon us at the rate of fifteen pounds to the square inch. Who can measure the mighty force of the I AM That I AM? It will not be denied. Sooner or later each individual recognizes its insistent knocking and opens the door that it may come in. And "eye hath not seen, nor ear heard, nor hath it entered into the heart of man," the glories awaiting him who opens himself to receive from his I AM.

The door through which I AM enters is in the upper brain. He does not enter as a person, or even as an idea, but rather as a stream of finest energy . . most positive energy.

The action of this stream of finest energy upon the already organized brain, refines it, dissolving and resolving its actual tissues into new Ideas. Ideas are organizations of thought force, and "thoughts are things"; that is, they are substantial just as the body is, only more so! . . namely, finer and more powerful.

What is conceived in the brain by the action of the I AM is sent out from the brain, through the nerve highways, into all the body. Being finer, and so positive, it acts upon the negative body tissues just as the I AM acts upon the brain; dissolving and resolving the tissues after its own pattern . . the "pattern given to thee in the mount"; the mountain, or head.

The highest intelligence in each individual is his most potent force; the thought conceived by the action of his I AM. It is the truth which the I AM has revealed to him. He has gained it through the "soul sense." It is the direct result of inspiration; the same kind of inspiration that we read about.

The I AM has always been speaking to us in this way; to every being on earth or in the heavens.

But, because of our limited intelligence, we have denied our highest thoughts as visionary and impractical. Thus we have ignorantly forbidden them to incarnate in the body. We have refused to receive the inspiration given us, not knowing its divine values.

We have so made for ourselves a prison of the actual. The actual has held us in its mighty womb, until we have grown to such proportions that we must be "born again" — "born from above."

"The whole creation groaneth and travaileth together in pain until the manifestation of the sons of God."

*"Oh, thou that pinest in the imprisonment of the Actual, and criest bitterly to the Gods for a kingdom wherein to rule*

*and create, know this of a truth, the thing thou seekest is already with thee, here or nowhere, couldst thou only see!"* — Thomas Carlyle.

Look up, Sweetheart, and see. Look up to the Ideals which are the source of all power; look out upon the Actual which is plastic to receive the impress of the Ideal. Behold the Omnipotent power which is at thy disposal, the realm in which thou mayest create!

Caleb went into the promised land because he "wholly followed the Lord his God." Upon the same principle, and only so, will we come into our promised land of immunity from disease of every form.

We must consciously rise to the Ideal realm, the highest, and live there. For what we think upon, we embody. We are what we have recognized; we shall be what we are recognizing today. We are choosing each moment either our highest or something less.

Our highest thought, persisted in will change any defect of temperament, and thus free us from disease and death. "Let patience have her perfect work."

**We have discovered that the father-mother of all** creation is man's I AMness. Man's consciousness is God. I AM conscious of the state. I AM the father-mother of all my ideas and my mind remains faithful to this new concept of self. My mind is disciplined. I take into that state the disciples, and I shut out of that state everything that would deny it.

**What is back of that success? A law as old as the hills,** a
law that has been known to psychologists for years . . the
law that the subconscious mind accepts as true anything
that is repeated to it convincingly and often. And once it has
accepted such a statement as true, it proceeds to mold the
Creative Force working through it in such wise as to MAKE
IT TRUE!

You see, where the conscious mind reasons inductively, the
subconscious uses only deductive reasoning. Where the
reasoning mind weighs each fact that is presented to it,
questions the truth or falsity of each, and then forms its
conclusions accordingly, the subconscious acts quite
differently. IT ACCEPTS AS FACT ANY STATEMENT THAT IS
PRESENTED TO IT CONVINCINGLY. Then, having accepted
this as the basis of its actions, it proceeds logically to do all
in its power to bring it into being.

That is why the two most important words in the English
language are the words . . "I AM." That is why the Ancients
regarded these two words as the secret name of God.

**The development of what may be termed the
consciousness** of soul, or the realization of the I AM and the
perfection of the I AM, will demonstrate conclusively to any
mind that the life of every individual is continuous and
endless; in fact, to become conscious of the I AM is to know
that the I AM and life are identical, and we know that life is
indestructible. Then add to this the great fact that you, the
real you, constitutes the I AM, and you have an exact basis
upon which you may demonstrate to yourself through pure
reason that you shall continue perpetually to live.

**As one realizes the allness of Mind as thinking Substance**
. . he "dwells in the secret place of the most High and abides under the shadow of the Almighty." Assert the fact that you are "Mind" in visible expression (pressed out) and no harm can come to you. This may be a long step for you but it is worthwhile.

The words in the Absolute . . Spirit, Mind, Life or Truth all mean the same thing. To select any one word and use it is sufficient to convey the desired knowledge. Christ gave the following definition of (I AM) God . . "God is Spirit", Since God is also Mind or Intelligence we may accept any of the following words as synonyms for the word "God": I AM, Life, Light, Love, Mind, Intelligence, Power, Spirit, Substance or Truth.

For the purpose of making clear to man the thought that I AM is Supply, I ask that the student remember that Mind also means Substance. When you say Mind is everywhere, you are also saying that Substance is everywhere.

**Jesus, when he stood up to read the prophecy** from Isaiah stating that someone would find the means by which this mind would be put in action, said: "This is finished," and closed the book. In other words, I can do it, I AM That mind made manifest. I can do all that that mind can do, (here is the greatest message to mankind), by admitting my desires and asking this mind, or Father, of whom I AM the son or expression, to do it for me. "Of myself (or the little intellect), I can do nothing; but the Father (or original desire of Spirit to express itself in action and form) doeth the works."

**God is Pure Spirit, Infinite Mind, and Infinite** Intelligence. The Bible calls the Name of God, "I AM," meaning Pure, Unconditioned Being. No one can, of course, define God, for God is Infinite, but there are certain Truths which the illumined of all ages have perceived as true of God, and that is why the Bible says, "I AM That I AM." What is "I AM?" It is your True Being . . your Real Self; nobody can say, "I AM," for you. That is the Presence of God in you, and your Real Identity. Whatever you affix to "I AM," and believe, you become. Always claim, "I AM strong, powerful, radiant, happy, joyous, illumined, and inspired"; then you are truly practicing the Presence, for all these qualities are true of God.

**He told his disciples that it was not necessary** to have a fancy name or a reason for a desire, that you wanted it, was sufficient. You need not put two cloaks on it, you need not refine it, or have gold in your purse; neither need you work for it, as symbolized by the brass. It is unnecessary for you to keep your mind on your DESIRE, for he said plainly that they were to rejoice when he left them, for "I go to prepare a place for you ... I will come again, and receive you unto myself; that where I AM, there ye may be also" . . or, the desire will manifest itself to you. But in the meantime "I will not leave you comfortless," for "the Holy Ghost (inspiration which I will send in my name . . DESIRE), he shall teach you all things;" or in other words, follow your hunch and it will lead you into your desire.

**Man must realize that he is one with I AM.** He cannot realize this as long as false beliefs fill his conscious mind. A vessel that is full cannot be filled. It can only be filled after it has been emptied. There is seemingly no room for ideas of Truth in the mind that is full of false thoughts. The "demons" (negative, false thoughts) must be driven out before healing of wrong conditions due to wrong mental states can take place.

As the student practices self-denial by denying the belief in separation from I AM, he will find it much easier to grasp the idea of Oneness with God. Denial is made by the human mind and in the human mind, for the human mind is denying itself. Think of the following and it will help you to see this point: The branches of a tree do nothing of themselves. We are mistaken if we say that they grow the leaves and produce the fruit. They can do nothing but keep in contact with the tree. If for one moment a branch were cut off from the trunk of the tree, its activity would cease. God as Universal Life, represents the sap in the tree flowing through all the branches. All mankind draws Power, Life, Mind and Intelligence from the same Source.

Man's lack of manifestation in the world of affairs, has been due to the fact that he has lacked in this . . he has not been conscious of his Oneness with I AM. Since we only have that of which we are conscious, you can understand that a lack of consciousness will mean a lack in manifestation. The bay is a part of the ocean, having the same water though it appears to be separated. The appearance does not affect the truth; the bay is always a part of the ocean, regardless as to appearance declaring otherwise. We may have the consciousness of our Oneness with God as we vibrate with God.

## I AM

**The words "I AM" are sacred as the divine name,** expressed completely as "I AM That I AM." This is the name of God.

Many people realize a more dynamic and positive power in affirmations based upon the Absolute or "I AM" than in statements expressed in the relative sense of becoming. For example, "I AM Life? "I AM Wisdom? "I AM Joy."

To understand this fully, realize that the affirmation is one of perfect truth concerning the real self, and that the ideal or model is lifted up to view for the purpose of actualizing it.

We must clearly understand that reality is synonymous with eternal perfection, and what we know as the actual represents the embodiment of the ideals represented in unfolding consciousness.

## I

The term "I" is usually employed to designate the actual person speaking. In the practice of absolute affirmation one uses the "I" in speaking as the real individual "in the image and likeness of God." As we continue to speak from this plane of consciousness, the qualities of the real "I" or individual are made more and more manifest in the personality.

## IDEAL

The ideal is the pattern in the consciousness of what we are to be, to do and to attract. As our ideals correspond more with the real and perfect, the actual conditions of life will be correspondingly transformed. We progress by advancing our ideals, and pressing forward with calm determination to realize them.

As the artist centers his mind on the model whose face or form he is to depict, so the attainment of the ideal consists of our concentrated attention upon the ideal.

Cherish the ideals of health, of happiness, of youth, of success. Be absolutely confident of their fulfillment. By causing our ideals to increase in power and beauty, our incentive and ability to live will grow accordingly. The world is primarily transformed through a change in the ideals of the people.

Ideal people and ideal environments are also attracted as we hold these ideals in mind.

## IMAGINATION

Imagination is the master power of visualization or picturing out of ideal desires, and living in the consciousness, for the time being, of their reality. Through this power one unfolds and grows to an Infinite degree. The right use of imagination makes men Gods and earth Heaven. All joys and all abilities follow the appropriate exercise of the power of imagination and the activities which the constructive imagination brings to fulfillment.

Through this power, one can rebuild his body and express health to the most inspiring degree. Radiant beauty can be realized, and also eternal youth of an ever-ascending quality. One can be original and creative, and express these qualities in superb discoveries and inventions.

Character can be molded; destiny can be made; success and fortune are assured through the genius of imagination.

Imagination is a most substantial force with power to make and remake the things about us. In due time, the cities of our nation will be absolutely transformed by the power of constructive and applied imagination. Every man, woman and child will be rich, healthful and happy.

**Unconditioned consciousness is God,** the one and only reality. By unconditioned consciousness is meant a sense of awareness; a sense of knowing that I AM, apart from knowing who I AM; the consciousness of being, divorced from that which I AM conscious of being. I AM aware of being man, but I need not be man to be aware of being. Before I became aware of being someone, I, unconditioned awareness, was aware of being, and this awareness does not depend upon being someone. I AM self-existent, unconditioned consciousness; I became aware of being someone; and I shall become aware of being someone other than this that I AM now aware of being; but I AM eternally aware of being whether I AM unconditioned formlessness or I AM conditioned form. As the conditioned state, I (man), might forget who I AM, or where I AM, but I cannot forget that I AM. This knowing that I AM, this awareness of being, is the only reality.

**Why must the new thought pattern be couched** in the present tense? Why do we say, "I AM PROSPERITY" instead of saying, "I SHALL BE PROSPEROUS"? Why must we claim something we do not have? Life always works in the present tense by direct affirmation. Jesus declared, "I AM This," or "I AM That," or "I AM The Other Thing," and immediately the thing decreed began to take form according to Law. To say that we shall be prosperous is well and good, but we are putting our prosperity off until some future time. To affirm our good in the present is to cause it to appear. Law, plus acceptance, plus belief is the pattern. If the idea of prosperity is to become a power in our lives, we must inwardly accept it as a present fact. Our thought, will, imagination, and feeling must agree with what we say.

**Say to yourself . .** "**I AM one with the Life Force** that runs the Universe, the great I AM of which Jesus said 'Before Abraham, was I AM.' I AM energy. I AM power. I AM filled with omnipotent life. The vitality of God permeates every fiber of my being. I AM well and whole in every part of my body. I AM made up of billions of cells of Intelligent Life, and that Intelligence is guiding me to Health and Happiness and Prosperity."

**I AM a law unto myself.**

Let us wake up to this law. Let us think of things as we want
them to be, not as they are.

Resolve now to do your own thinking. Be the divine thinker
of your own thoughts. No one else must do your thinking for
you. No one else must splash his ideas all over you, all over
your mind, for you to work out. If someone is making you
unhappy, start a different trend (your own trend) of thinking.
Go within your chamber of mind as frequently as necessary
and know that no one has the power to make you unhappy
unless you accept the idea and permit it to take root in you.
"No weapon that is formed against thee shall prosper; and
every tongue that shall rise against thee in judgment thou
shalt condemn. This is the heritage of the servants of the
Lord, and their righteousness is of me, saith the Lord." Think
happiness and happiness will come to you. You are the way
to your own happiness. I AM happy, creates happiness. You
can think the happy idea and soon you will find happiness
about you. The Force is the Great Servant. It works out the
ideas we give to it. You need no longer be bound to lack if
you will live with the idea of plenty. You need no longer be
deaf if you will live with the idea of hearing.

**I AM That I AM is one of the principal Bible** terms for God. It means unconditioned Being. It means the great Creative Power that is absolutely unlimited. It is an attempt . . and a very successful one . . to express, as far as language can, the infinity of God.

"I AM" means you . . the individual. It is an assertion or affirmation of existence and needs to be qualified in some way. We say, for example, "I AM a man" or "I AM a woman," "I AM an American" or "I AM a Spaniard," "I AM a lawyer" or "I AM a baker," "I AM a Republican" or "I AM a Democrat." In each case we state an important fact about ourselves, and to that extent we limit ourselves . . not in a negative sense, but in a positive and constructive sense.

If I AM an American, I AM not a Spaniard; if I AM a man, I AM not a woman, etc.

Now I AM is absolutely unlimited, and the only phrase which can express this is I AM That I AM. I AM . . what? I AM . . pure unconditioned being, unlimited, and unspecified in any way. To affirm that I AM is any particular thing would imply limitation, or at least a circumscription, and God is unlimited.

It is man's business to be something in particular, and not to try to be everything, because he is an individualization. If you struck all the notes in the scale together you would only have confused noise. Music consists in the selection and special groupings of certain notes.

In God's universe each one of us has his place and it is our business to find that true place and express it . . to play our part correctly in the great orchestra. God, however, is the Great Conductor and the whole orchestra too, unlimited and without beginning and without end.

**"Thy will be done on earth as it is in Heaven,"** God's will for you is for riches, for happiness, for health. If you haven't these now, deny the lack. Deny the wrong conditions. Say to yourself . . "There is no lack in Heaven. There is no disease there, no weakness, no trouble or conflict, no worries of any kind. There is only love and plenty."

Then take your beliefs out of the images around you, which are merely the result of your previous belief objectified and put all your faith, all your hopes, all your strength and abilities into making your new Heaven images come true.

You CAN do it. But you must believe so firmly that you can actually ACT the part. As the Prophet Noel told us "Let the weak say . . I AM strong!" And the poor say, I AM rich. And the sick say, I AM well. And the miserable say, I AM happy. Say it, repeat it until you believe it . . then ACT the part!

**I AM is the perfect and full expression** of invisible Spirit. It is the Universal Mind in action. I AM is health. I AM is prosperity. I AM is success. The I AM is the Principle and Power of God and the invisible power of man. What we call your mind and my mind are two manifestations or expressions of the One Mind. We do not say you have "an air" and I have "an air," or that a fish has "a water." There is one water in which fishes live; one air which we breathe; one Mind of which we are all a part.

**Concepts are the most difficult to overcome.** Even a concept of ourselves, no matter how great that concept may be, is a limitation. Let us get this straight otherwise you will not receive the benefit of the teachings of the Masters. A concept of yourself no matter how great it may be is a limitation. Therefore we want no concepts of ourselves. Why, our minds must be entirely and completely free. What the Masters mean by that is this: you cannot conceive how mighty you are. You cannot conceive the Infinite Spirit in a concept. When you make a concept of yourself you have created an image or an idea of yourself, as it were, in the mind, and it must remain such, and as that concept grows and solidifies there is no longer any progress because what you think you are. Therefore we want no concepts of ourselves. We want the freedom of knowing that I AM. Nothing else than knowing that I AM!

**"I AM Alpha and Omega, the beginning and the end,** saith the Lord." Our ideal murmuring in our hearts is the alpha; in order that it become the omega, we must enter into the feeling that it is ours now, and walk the earth knowing that it is so. Failure to realize our desire over a long period of time results in frustration and unhappiness. I have talked to many men in different parts of the country; their frequent complaint is that for years they have tried in vain to attain a certain ideal or position in life, and that they have failed miserably. They did not know that the desire to be, to do, and to have was the Still Small Voice speaking to them, and all that was necessary was for them to say, "Yes, Father, I accept and believe it"; then walk the earth knowing that, "It is done."

**To mold these surroundings to our liking is the secret** of Mental Science which these lessons are attempting to unravel. We have been helpless because we did not know our strength . . not because we did not possess strength. Strength has been latent within us, and so has health, because Omnipresent Being (I AM) is in everything, constantly developing from negative to positive . . and constantly asserting a riper unfoldment of its own enormous vitality. But only knowledge could make us aware of this, and the knowledge was lacking.

The law is the great I AM. It existed always, and may be had for the perceiving. The first step toward the appropriation of truth is to recognize it. This is the fulfilling of the first injunction: "Believe, if you would be saved." Belief is recognition. It is the wakening of the intelligence to a perception of truth. To recognize a truth is to believe it. After believing . . recognition . . what then? To him that overcometh are all the promises given. And that which we are to overcome is our former habit of unbelief in the omnipotence and omnipresence of Eternal Being (I AM). To climb high enough in the scale of intelligence to perceive that a truth is a truth, is to place that truth within our reach; and is recognition. To then bring our will-power into operation, and by its operation to overcome our former unbeliefs that conflict with the acceptance of the new truth, this will make that truth our own; and is appropriation. We grow step by step in this mighty magnet . . the universe . . by recognition and appropriation of truth. We have now come up far enough in the light of our constantly increasing intelligence to recognize a very great truth, indeed . . the truth that in all the universe there is no evil, nothing but absolute Life or Being; and because we have at last recognized this master truth, we are called upon to bring all our past beliefs under review and judge them by a stronger light than they were ever subjected to before.

**Now that we understand that the Universal Mind** is always "pressing out" into visibility, we know that things are thoughts and thoughts are things. When the student not only believes this with the conscious mind but knows it, he is then one with the Source of all supply. As long as the mind believes that Spirit and matter exist as separated parts of the whole, there is bound to be confusion. If there is confusion in the mind, there is struggle and with struggle comes the lack of peace, relaxation and harmony. When man is convinced that there is one Mind, he becomes more harmonious and as a result has more Wisdom. When this same individual knows that there is one Substance and that he must therefore be a part of it, he becomes more harmonious with Supply and has more of the good things of life classified under the word "prosperity."

To realize prosperity then, is to realize I AM as the Substance of all things. To this end we must stop believing that matter means another Substance. That which is called matter is really a different form or manifestation of I AM. The reason all things do not look alike is due to the fact that they are vibrating at different rates. A tree has its rate of vibration; so has a rock, and if the rock vibrated at the same rate as the tree, it would no longer be a rock in appearance, but a tree. The elimination of belief in matter must take place before the student is really on the highway to success. Probably more people have been confused over this word "matter" than over anything else. In the light of present day science it is easily understood and when comprehended places one's feet on the road to abundance.

**WE must resolutely set our faces to the rising**
consciousness of the Son of Truth; seeing only the One
Power we must destroy the adversary and leave the field to
God or Good. All that is in any way negative must be wiped
off the slate and we must daily come into the higher thought,
to be washed clean of the dust and chaos of the objective life.
In the silence of the soul's communion with the Great Cause
of All Being, into the stillness of the Absolute, into the secret
place of the Most High, back of the din and the ceaseless
roar of life, we shall find a resting place and a place of real
spiritual power. Speak in this inner silence and say, "I AM
one with the Almighty; I AM one with all life, with all power,
with all presence. I AM, I AM, I AM." Listen to the silence.
From out of the seeming void the voice of peace will answer
the waiting soul, "All is well."

**The Universal Law offers to each one of us satisfaction** in
all our ways; and that we remain unsatisfied is not the fault
of the Law. That we do not know how to obtain this
satisfaction is not an injustice of the great First Cause, but is
rather a matter of indifference or choice on our part. Either
we have not cared enough about obtaining our birthright to
determine to know how it may be obtained, or we have
chosen to spend our time and effort for other purposes than
learning, first, what is the truth; and second, in living that
truth at the cost of all things else. The Law opens the door to
us freely in its "I AM the way, and the truth and the life," and
we may study it at will. But, the Almighty does not force us
to know the truth, or to live it, if we know it, in order that we
may have the freedom that is ours at any time we have
earned the right to have it. Concentrated right thinking is the
sure prophecy of its own fulfillment; and this ought to be
sufficient incentive to decide all of us to get acquainted with
the working power of the mental realm.

**To understand what it means to be in the absolute state,** or even to imagine the existence of such a state, we shall find it necessary to give much thought to the very highest states of consciousness; and, although we may not always be able to form a perfect conception of the absolute state of perfect being, still we can form mental conceptions that are so similar to that state that they will give us, for the time being, an indication to how and where we should turn attention. And here we should remember that although we may become conscious of perfect being, that does not mean that we have become conscious of all there is in perfect being. Such a consciousness would require an eternity; but we can become conscious of perfect being; we can draw so near to the absolute state that we can form a clear conception of the life of the absolute. However, we can never become conscious of all that is in the absolute, because again, that would require an eternity.

It is true that all who are spiritually awakened are conscious more or less of the absolute, and there are times when they can draw so near to perfect being that they can really feel that they are in reality the I AM. And here you should remember that whenever you can feel that you and the I AM are one and the same, then you are in absolute consciousness. However, you may continue to penetrate more and more deeply into that state for eternity, and the more deeply you penetrate into that state the larger the I AM becomes in your conscious understanding.

**It is in the heart of Being that man says "I AM."** It is the I AM of man that is ever one with the Father, as one with God as a drop of water is one with the ocean of which it is a part. Man's being is one with the Being of God and is within itself that which God is. For this reason, man within himself is power, substance and intelligence. It is knowing this that gives him dominion in the realm of form, or makes all form subject to him. "Even the winds and the waves obey him," they said of Jesus, who was the first to claim his God-given right of dominion in earth.

Within the heart of man's consciousness lies the creative law through which he expresses his Being. This is the treasure in heaven of which Jesus spoke, and is a treasure because within it lies the power of bringing forth every earthly treasure. It is the cause of things. It is a trinity principle, and through its use "All things are possible," for within it lies the power and substance and intelligence through which all things are created.

This heart of Being, man's Spirit, or Christ self, may be understood as follows:

1. Wisdom, or Power to express.
2. Love, or Substance with which to express.
3. Truth, or Intelligence with which to conceive what shall be expressed.

It can be readily seen that when in man lies all power to express, and all substance with which to express, and all intelligence with which to think what form shall be expressed, there remains but one thing necessary to bring forth expression, and that is to decide what form shall be thought into expression, or to intelligently conceive what the power and substance of Being shall produce. This definite decision as to what shall be expressed is like choosing a seed for sun and earth to bring forth. They are willing to produce any harvest man desires, but he himself must decide what he wishes to sow. Even so, power and substance lie within the being of man and will bring forth into expression that which he conceives, or prophesies, if he will only fulfill the law of mind, which is the law of faith, by "Asking" for what he wants and by believing he has that for which he asks.

"What things soever ye desire, when ye pray, believe ye receive them, and ye shall have them."

We will now consider the four planes of man's being again, understanding that in his heart, or Spirit, is the power and substance and intelligence to bring all form into manifestation; That in soul the Prophet is always asking "WHAT shall be brought forth?" That in mind the law is to be fulfilled, or the individual is to believe he has that which he has conceived, since he indeed does have it in unmanifest form, and that through believing he has, he actually comes to have in expression that which previously he had only in Being.

In the Heart of man's being, where he is one with the Father, the Father says, "I AM That power, substance and intelligence which is the fulfillment of your every desire." In Soul, the question is asked, "What do you desire?" In Mind, it is required, "Believe ye have that which ye desire." In Expression, it is promised, "And ye shall have the fulfillment of your desire."

**As STUDENTS of LIFE, we are seeking a method** by means of which we can attain more Good. What we all want is to eliminate friction and anxiety. We desire health of body, peace of mind, and success in all of our affairs. This is possible through the harmonious adjustment of the mind to the outer and inner realm. The fear and worry of life can be banished in no other way than by Understanding. To become enlightened and to realize the Truth is to find your Self-reliance increased. "Understanding," in the sense in which I AM using the word, includes our individual relationship to the universal Reality. The moment we look upon the Universe as the WHOLE, of which we are a part, we feel an alliance with a friendly Power. The Universe is not a foe to be conquered, but a friend to be understood.

**It is said that most of Mind (nine-tenths),** like the iceberg, is submerged. Just because you cannot see yourself does not mean that you do not exist. An iceberg is often seen floating against the current. This is explained by what I have just said . . that it is nine-tenths submerged. One-tenth is seen in the current flowing north but it is buried so far down that nine-tenths of it is in another current going in the opposite direction. Many people are able to go against the current of events, and succeed. They are called the strong souls. They are strong, however, because they understand that they are not the visible man but the invisible "I AM."

**Dear friends, you who at times feel almost discouraged,** you who are being continually "sand-papered" by the petty worries and anxieties of life, just try for one week always saying the I AM upward, toward the good, and see what the result will be. Instead of saying, "I AM afraid it will rain," say, "I hope it will not rain;" instead of "I AM sorry," say, "I would have been glad had it been so and so;" instead of saying, "I AM weak and cannot accomplish," say, "I AM, because Thou art; I can accomplish, because I AM." You will be astonished at the result.

**Mind of itself has no power, therefore mind has no power over you.** Although you create images in your mind and then fear them, it is like fearing your own shadow. Neither has matter any power of its own; it is but mind modified. When you understand this you will get behind form to that which is. You then become one with the Creator; not creating imperfection, but manifesting that which is already perfect within you. The Impersonal becomes the personal, and we see the Spiritual World before us. The I AM of the ego disappears, and the I AM That I AM appears. When you say knowingly . . I AM That I AM, all things will respond; the elements will obey you; anything will be possible to you. The world will be negative to you, and you will be positive to everything in it. The Master said, "All power has been given unto me in heaven and on earth."

**Everything in the universe has come from something.** It was believed at one time that something was made out of nothing. This is not scientific and therefore not true. All things in the visible universe are made of something and that something is invisible to our physical sense of sight. The invisible becomes visible by mental activity. In the past, many people believed what I have just stated, but could not seem to manifest in the visible by the action of mind. The difficulty is here: they believed that mind was over matter, and that mind could work with matter and form it, but the results were very disappointing. When you understand the nature of matter you will not experience a repetition of the past. That which is called matter is in reality Spirit, and it is absolutely necessary that you accept this. The natural science point of view regarding matter will possibly help you most, because it fits in best with your preconceived ideas. The present scientific position is that matter and electricity are synonymous terms.

The basis of the so-called material universe consists of lines of force. I believe that what the scientist calls lines of force, correspond to what we call thought. Since matter is one with thought, it is thought brought into visibility. You will see from this, that a man's thoughts may become the things he sees and feels.

Since there is no matter, the more we can eliminate the material thought, the nearer we are to Reality. All is Spirit; then Spirit produces form out of itself. As one understands Substance, one reaches the realization of Reality. Formerly, the idea in the minds of most people was that Substance was matter. Now that you know that matter is nothing as matter, then matter understood is Substance expressed. Stop here again and think. The Substance of all is Spirit. The word "substance" (from sub, under and stare, to stand) means "that which stands under." That which stands under the form of the thing you see and want is Spirit.

One might say then, "What I really want is more Spirit Substance." I reply, "No. It is the consciousness of this, that you want."

Let me give you a simple illustration. It being true that things and conditions are thoughts expressed, why do not people think rain during a drought? If they should, rain would appear. The difficulty is that they think the thing they do not want into manifestation, and then complain when they get it. The old prayer meetings conducted in the interest of those who wanted rain were very successful. This was true because the people stopped thinking drought (lines of force producing what they thought) and changed their mental action through getting into a universal, impersonal consciousness. Then the divine Power had an opportunity of expressing Itself through them as rain (lines of force producing electrons, electrons producing atoms and atoms forming into molecules of moisture).

The material thought that Substance is material, has been responsible for "short circuiting" our health, wealth and happiness. Because matter can be seen, men have thought that it was different from the primary (unseen) Substance. There is only one Substance. As we have this in mind we will eliminate the dual belief, and thus cease being double-minded.

As a great scientist has said, "Reality is Permanence." Spirit is the only Reality, and since there is no matter, but all is Spirit . . visible and invisible . . Spirit as Substance never changes. When one speaks of changing his mind he means that he has changed the action of mind, or stopped thinking one way and thought in another. Spirit (Substance;

Permanence) never changes, but the form of it may change from one expression into another. As one understands this action, one can see how true scientific thinking (guided by a teacher, perhaps) changes the form of what has been called illness, poverty and unhappiness into health, wealth and happiness.

Many people succeed in attaining the thing they want, wholly unconscious of the law by which they attain it. This being true does not release the many who have suffered because they did not know. It is better to know the law, and consciously apply it in realizing the thing we want: By this understanding one may say, "I AM creator and not creature."

You now have made up your mind definitely as to what you want. The desire indicates that it is for you, or you would not desire it. You must now state that you have what you desire. Just here do not think that it is too vague. You have not the thing you want in form, but you have it in Substance. You want form. Remember, if you expect results, you must keep each link in the chain, or the chain (law) will be broken. Know what form you want of the Substance you have. If there is any doubt as to whether you have Substance, go back and read carefully. You are not ready for the treatment until you have this understanding.

Consider this brief outline in three steps:

1. Know what you want.
2. State what you want.
3. State that you have it in Substance.

Up to the present moment, it is very necessary that you have understanding. You cannot expect direct results if you simply recite the formula; you must understand it. Be patient and do not think it is impractical. Remember . . it is a science; in fact it is this science which the ancients understood so well.

When I speak of the "consciousness of Plenty" I do not mean that you must know that there is plenty of money, business, or any other form, but there is an abundance of Substance out of which forms come. Be sure that you understand this, or the statement, "There is Plenty " will be but words.

Let me give you a few simple, practical illustrations. A woman may have the material to make a dress, without having the dress in form. She is pleased to know that there is sufficient material out of which to make the dress. I walked into a bakery sometime ago, and while there was not a loaf of bread in the store, there was plenty of dough to be made into loaves, back in the bakeshop. The student may at this point ask this question . . "Would the dress or loaves of bread come into form unless someone made them?" I answer, "No; but no one could do it without Mind." You must not be idle and wait passively for all things to come to you without effort. Your thoughts form your Good and you will have success as directed by Mind. Then there is your constructive thought that will lead someone else to respond to what you think, and you will reap the benefit.

I will state with authority that as you develop the consciousness of Plenty (plenty of Substance), you will be magnetic and attract many desirable things in an unconscious way.

"To him that hath [understanding] shall be given, and to him that hath not [understanding] shall be taken away even that which he hath.

From this point on I shall use the word "God" in place of Substance. This will spiritualize your mind and act in neutralizing the materialistic thought. Your success will be measured largely by the degree in which you eliminate the material thought. The following is very helpful in enlarging the consciousness: "Sensing the allness of God, leaving out all trace of human personality, if earnestly engaged in, will permanently remove every difficulty from my path"

The difficulty with many people is mental limitation. You may reasonably expect forms in proportion to your capacity to receive them. To illustrate, it is not likely that you will receive five hundred dollars a week, if you are expecting twenty-five.

Wealth is created mentally first. The stream of Plenty will not flow toward the stingy, parsimonious thought. Holding the poverty thought keeps one in touch with poverty producing conditions. You are a center and according to your thought you receive.

Again let me remind you that an expanded mentality means an expanded and enlarged life of plenty. To declare that there is plenty of God (Substance) is to declare a fact that will manifest.

The thought of "Allness" will so enlarge a man's conception of life, that narrowness gives way to broadness, intolerance to tolerance, hate to love, illness to health, failure to success and lack to plenty. While you have been studying the subject matter herein presented, your mind has been clarified. As the mental fog of negation has disappeared, it has left you with the faculty so clear and sharp, that it creates and attracts even now.

This is a study, and as you have grasped the idea, the mental law has been put into operation because of the renewing effect which this has had upon the mind. The word "consciousness" has appeared frequently. I want to make this plain to the reader. By it, I mean to be aware of or awake to the real fact . . not to the seeming. When you are aware that the thing you want is in reality Mind Substance expressed, and that you make that form by mental activity, it is "consciousness."

Just here the student may still be in doubt as to the process. If this question is in the mind . . "Since I have the Substance and have furnished the pattern or mold by knowing definitely what I want, must I not work in some way to put that Substance into form, and if so, how?"

I will answer it. I repeat that you will be active and not wait for things to come to you (though they will), but you will not be active in the sense of being conscious of working for the thing. It is not necessary to visualize and work mentally, but to realize the "Allness of God," and let the law operate and the mind work out your form. This may be different from anything you have been taught heretofore, but observation, experience and testimonies from many, have convinced me that this is the unfailing Absolute.

By the other method (visualizing) one becomes too conscious of the material thought, instead of letting the power operate.

There is a great deal of electrical power along the wires in our homes. There is enough there to run a motor, or only give a 25 watt bulb power. It is according to our understanding. A story is told of a woman who had been using the old carbon globes and seemed perfectly satisfied. One day an enterprising agent advised her to use his bulb that would give much better illumination. He screwed the bulb into the socket and the room was filled with light. The woman was surprised and asked how this was done. The agent replied that there was an abundance of this power in the wire, but that she had not been using it. She had a 25 watt bulb consciousness and received just that much. The missing link that connects the abundance of Substance with the manifestation is to know . . "There is plenty of God." Remember . . the bulb did not form the electricity or make it, but acted as a medium.

Let me tell you what you may expect from this study. As the mind expands under the influence of this idea of Abundance, there will be a breaking up of the old ideas of poverty and lack. As these are "broken up under the positive influence of the Truth, outer conditions will also break up and outer circumstances will improve. The payment of money long deferred will take place; new customers will visit your store; new opportunities for gain will come into your professional life; you will find it easier to make sales. People will be attracted toward you and your circle of friends will be widened; money will come easily and freely. People will seem more kind, not competing with you, but instead cooperating. All things will work together for good in your behalf in the outer world, because you have a new inner world.

When things change, know that it is the working of this Law that cannot fail Any idea held in the mind will be realized and demonstrated. The reason for poverty producing conditions and circumstances is that the thought of lack has been retained in the mind and eventually realized. With this new idea and understanding of "Plenty " we accept the fixed idea and repeat it often with understanding: "There is Plenty."

One final suggestion here at this point do not think "plenty of money," "plenty of positions," "plenty of friends" . . but "plenty of I AM."

**The greatest discovery ever made was the discovery** of
the creative power of thought, because upon this hinges
man's entire evolution. The ability to affirm, to say "I AM," to
be conscious of one's relationship to the Universe, is not only
a guarantee that man Is, and is some part of the Universe, it
is itself a proclamation of the Universe, since the only
knowledge of God we can have must come through the
consciousness of man. The consciousness of man is an
extension of the consciousness of God.

**The difference between an ordinary man** and a God-man
is that the God-man knows he IS while the other does not
know. The Power of the Truth can only be established when
we free our minds from all concepts and preconceived ideas.
The Truth will then set us free, and, although we live in the
world of phenomena and shadows, we are not bound by it. "I
AM not of this world," the Master said. Do you believe then
that you are born of the flesh? If you do then you are already
dead. If you believe that you are born of the Spirit you
already now have Eternal Life; you have passed across from
death to life. Do you not see that you cannot make Truth
conform to any idea, any creed, any dogma, any system or
philosophy! Can you not understand that you cannot make
Truth conform to anything! That has been your trouble all
along.

**So when you say, "I AM poor, sick or weak; I AM not one with the Creative Mind,"** you are using that creative power to keep yourself away from the Infinite; and just as soon as you declare that you are one with God, there is a rushing out to meet you, as the Father rushed out to meet the prodigal son. "The Spirit seeketh," but as long as your mind thinks in the terms of conditions you cannot overcome. The difficulty comes from our inability to see our own Divine nature, and its relation to the Universe. Until we awake to the fact that we are one in nature with God, we will not find the way of life; until we realize that our own word has the power of life we will not see the way of life; and this brings us to the consideration of the use of the Word in our lives.

**It is all a part of the injunction, "Seek ye first the Kingdom,** etc.," for you cannot find the Kingdom until you are able to control those forces of your emotional and mental nature that heretofore had their way with you almost unopposed. If and when you are able to command, "Be Still, and know I AM," and be instantly obeyed on all planes of consciousness, then and then only will you be able to do the work that will be given you; for then only can you work in the Consciousness and with the Power of Christ . . the Master within.

**There is always Substance enough to make more than you ever desired,** but you have to believe in more than you see and that all things visible have come out of the invisible. We are walking through this invisible something"; living in it; breathing it; thinking into it; talking into it and according to our thoughts and words shall the Substance be formed. The material is here. If you think negatively, you will have negative results. If you think and speak positively into this universal Substance, you will have positive results.

Since this world moves . . and it moves at the rate of 17 miles a minute from west to east . . since there is "this something" which fills full the whole universe, how can this world move through "that something" without friction; without being consumed? Because it is porous and in this porous state this ether flows through the world as the latter revolves through it. Ether must be more rigid than steel and lighter than air. Every point in this study is scientific, true and practical. As we accept the fact that Substance surrounds us wherever we move and this Substance is Mind . . and as we apply the laws of right thinking and think and speak into it, we shall have whatsoever we desire.

We have heard much of the fourth dimension and we have vainly endeavored to understand it. In my opinion it is "consciousness." It is invisible to our sense of sight, but nevertheless real. In man's evolution, the day may come when he will recognize ten or more dimensions. To make this very plain, consider the following simple illustration:

A caterpillar is crawling on the top of a table. Imagine that he was born there, for the table is one in the naturalist's study. The caterpillar has seen nothing of the world but that flat table top. He therefore lives in a world of two dimensions: length and breadth. He crawls to the edge of the table and looks over and discovers something new. The new discovery is a third dimension. He discovers for the first time that the table has depth. It was always there but the caterpillar did not know it. Now if I stand over the table and drop bits of food, the caterpillar will see them but will probably be unable to account for them, since they did not come from any one of the three dimensions. They came from some unseen but real source, called the fourth dimension.

When we are able to hold in our consciousness the idea of "the invisible abundant Substance everywhere," we are really living mentally in the fourth dimension and bringing it into manifestation in the visible world.

We are intelligent beings, to be sure, endowed with intelligence, but most of humanity is still living in a world of three dimensions . . length, width and depth. Has it ever occurred to you that the third dimension (depth) is a matter of faith? You look at a cube and you can see two dimensions, but you accept the third (thickness) on faith. You cannot look through the cube but because you judge its weight you conclude that it is solid. But there is more than we can see and if we accept the third dimension by faith, why not accept the fourth?

It was Christ who believed in the fourth dimension (I AM, consciousness) when he looked at the three dimensional loaves and fishes and then realized the fourth (abundance of the invisible Substance) and fed five thousand. All scientific data today is being brought forth in support of spiritual truths. The following proves this to be true (once more we come to God in the language of our day): Mr. Einstein hinted at the possibility of light being deflected by the "pull" of the sun. Of course if this were true it would prove that light must have some weight and as a very high vibration is Substance.

In the history of science, the year 1919 will long be remembered. The British astronomers who went to Africa to observe the eclipse of the sun on May 19, 1919, came back with the proof that a ray of light passing near the sun is bent out of its straight course. The photographs taken during the six minutes when the sun was shadowed, show the surrounding stars in different positions from those in which they are seen when the sun's disk is not in their midst. This shows that a ray of light from a star is refracted or bent as it passes close to the sun and confirms Einstein's theory that light is affected by gravitation.

The old sun worshipers of the past were not so far from Truth when they looked to the sun as their Source of Supply. "I AM . . the Light." "Walk in the Light." "Every good gift and every perfect gift is from above [fourth dimension], and cometh down from Father of Lights, with whom is no variableness, neither shadow of turning."

There is plenty of Substance. The following is from Henry Ford's paper, the Dearborn Independent: If you can imagine a world in which the source of supply will be so plentiful that people will worry about not using enough of it, instead of worrying as we do now, about using too much, you will have a picture of the world that is soon to be. We have long depended on the resources which Nature long ago stored up; the resources which can be exhausted. We are entering an era when we shall create resources which shall be constantly renewed, so that the only loss will be not to use them. There will be such a plenteous supply of heat, light and power that it will be sin not to use all we want.

This era is coming in now." Mind is not the Supplier, but the Supply . . the Substance of the thing itself. Man may now know that as he realizes the Substance (that which stands under the thing), he may have the form of the thing. There is Plenty. There is plenty of Substance.

**"I AM the vine, ye are the branches."**

**A branch has no life save it be rooted in the vine.** All I need do to change the fruit is to change the vine. You have no life in my world save that I AM conscious of you. You are rooted in me and, like fruit, you bear witness of the vine that I AM.

There is no reality in the world other than your consciousness. Although you may now seem to be what you do not want to be, all you need do to change it, and to prove the change by circumstances in your world, is to quietly assume that you are that which you now want to be, and in a way you do not know you will become it. There is no other way to change this world. "I AM the way." My I AMness, my consciousness is the way by which I change my world. As I change my concept of self, I change my world.

When men and women help or hinder us, they only play the part that we, by our concept of self, wrote for them, and they play it automatically. They must play the parts they are playing because we are what we are. You will change the world only when you become the embodiment of that which you want the world to be. You have but one gift in this world that is truly yours to give and that is yourself. Unless you yourself are that which you want the world to be, you will never see it in this world.

**Apply this principle to the affirmation, I AM PROSPERITY,** and you will see how wealth comes out in your affairs. Whatever you believe becomes. Whatever you think expresses. You build your Consciousness with your I AM, by the things you think and do all day long. As a man thinketh in his I AM, so are his circumstances. Do you grasp that principle, you who are looking for better jobs, more income, greater freedom? If you do, the circumstances in your life will have to change. Did you ever stop to consider why it is that a man who has made a fortune and lost it can make another one faster than the man who never had one? It is because his Consciousness is greased in that direction. Do you know why many businesses disintegrate and fall apart when their founders die? It is because the supporting Consciousness has been taken away. If we can show you what is wrong with your thinking, that knowledge should constitute the greater part of the cure for you.

One of the reasons people fail to demonstrate sufficient income is that they imagine something other than I AM is their Source of Supply. Another reason is that they try to build prosperity without I AM. We cannot function from the Source (center) of Supply without Him. Those who do not understand this will try to change outer circumstances without changing their Consciousness . . a process exactly like trying to lift one's self by one's own boot straps. It is important to make up your mind about the things you wish to demonstrate, but it is more important to be willing to change your mind in order to get them. "Of mine own self, I can do nothing."

"The Father that dwelleth in me, He doeth the works." The way is clear. The more you forget self and rely on I AM, the greater your demonstration will be. Metaphysics teaches you but one thing: How to be a good insulator through which the Power can flow. "I, if I be lifted up from the earth, will draw all men [manifestation] unto Me." When the I AM is lifted up, your lack is turned into plenty. Do you begin to sense the riches that will be poured into your life when this adjustment has been made?

**From the standpoint of the body these statements will of course appear to be untrue,** but here we should remember that the truth, when viewed from the false standpoint, always seems false. When we affirm these statements, however, we are not speaking of the body. We are speaking of the soul, the spirit, the real you, the "I AM" and if you will analyze the nature of the soul or the "I AM," you will find that the above statements, when applied to the soul, are absolutely true. Always remember that you are the soul. The body is your instrument. The body is therefore dependent upon you, the soul, for all its conditions; and the conditions of the body, be they health or disease, happiness or distress, power or weakness all are results of what you think.

As long as you think the untruth, evil and wrong conditions will appear in your body. There will be disease, poverty, distress, misfortune, and the like; but as soon as you learn to think the truth, those conditions will disappear and good conditions will manifest in the body instead. There will be health, happiness, plenty, peace, comfort, harmony, wisdom and power.

The soul, or the "I AM," already has within itself everything that is good, and if you would have all of these good things from within express themselves in your personality, you must think and live right. You must think the truth and think it constantly.

**"I AM surrounded by pure Spirit, by God,** the Living Spirit. My thought is God thought, and it is the law unto that thing where unto it is spoken. Everything that I do shall be a success. I AM led, guided and inspired by the Living Spirit of Love and of right action. I AM compelled to move in the right direction and to always know what to do, where, and how to do it. "I AM surrounded by right action. I AM filled with the consciousness of right action. Right action is success in all that I undertake to do. I AM successful in all my undertakings, and I AM compensated for all my efforts. I AM surrounded by Substance, which is always taking the form of supply and always manifesting Itself to me in the form of whatever my need may be at the time. "I always have an abundance of money and an abundance of whatever it takes to make life happy and opulent.

There is a continuous movement toward me of supply, of money, of all that I need to express the fullest life, happiness and action. "I have an inner understanding of my place in the Universe. I know that it is unique. The Divine has not incarnated in anyone else in just the same individual way that It has in me. I AM unique and forever individualized. Therefore, I do not need to imitate anyone or to long for the good, that belongs to another. All good is now mine and is now manifest in my experience. I do not compete with anyone, for I AM and remain forever myself. This self is united with all selves, but is always an individual and a unique self. "The opportunity for self-expression and compensation is always open to me and I AM at all times compelled to know, accept and operate upon this opportunity. I have abundance because I AM abundance. "All that the Father hath is mine"

**Love is the greatest power in the universe.** It opens all doors, breaks down all barriers of class or creed. All recognize love, in whatever form it comes, and through whomsoever it manifests. Love cannot be gainsaid. With love, the divine attribute, in your soul you can do all things, and without love you can do nothing. The secret of the Christ power and healing was divine love manifest in the flesh. All races, all sects, all cults, all religions look to God as a God of love, and the secret of the Christ power over people of all classes, rich and poor, Jew or Gentile, Pharisee and Sadducee was His divine love.

His divine love and compassion radiating out to bless the world, instilled faith in the multitudes who recognized the God-like quality in him, and it healed them. There is only one path to travel if you would climb the heights of illumination, and that is the path of Love. Let the love flowing from the Father radiate through you to bless others in turn, and you will find your reward. Behold, I stand at the door and knock. I AM divine love. I would teach thee wisdom. I would awake the dormant faculties of thy soul. I would illuminate thy mind and body and spirit with Divine love that it may shed a greater brilliance on the world. I AM knocking gently. Wilt thou let me in?

**Examine your sayings and see if they are superficial,** and if you find they are, there is no depth to them. You say them in parrot fashion, that is why they do not live. When you recognize this mighty truth, the realization of it gives you control, and everything obeys you, The elements respond to your call, and form according to the image held with this understanding. I know this to be true. On several occasions it has been done. Examine your mind, examine your faith! Do you believe it? No, of course, if you do not believe it so it will not be to you, because of the creative power.

1. Creative Power . . that is your Consciousness. First cause; the Reality in God, Reality in man. The Consciousness of God individualized in man becomes one with the Creative Power. Whatever you do with this Creative Power so it must be unto You. That is the only Creative Power there is, unlimited in its nature.

2. Thoughts, Images . . you create a thought and you live in the thought you create. You live in the image you create. You do not know that you have created it. You have tremendous power yet you know it not.

3. Manifestation of Belief . . Now, creative power, creates secondary cause and effect . . you are living in these two but you are not really living at all. You are living in your images and the manifestation of your images. As your images manifest you set up a tremendous emotion of fear which has no more power than you give it because you believe in the illusion you create. There is no limitation to your thinking, there is no limitation to the creative power in you. Whatever you think, so it must be unto you. And this is the Law of your being. How tremendous it is! I AM the Life. Try and grasp the meaning . . I AM the Life. I AM the Creative Power. What I think must manifest. My thoughts may be double . . now I have it, now I do not have it.

**"I AM the Way . . the only way you can travel** . . either without or within; for only by using My power can you be, can you express, can you do, can you go. Hence only by finding and knowing Me as your true and only self, can you ever find the Kingdom. "I AM the Truth. There would be no knowing in you if it were not for Me in you. For am I not the Interpreter . . the only Teacher of Truth . . the only Knower . . for you? "I AM the Life. There would be no life in your body if I were not dwelling in it . . for I AM the Life that lives it. I AM the Life of God that flows into, centers in you, expresses you, and Is you. "Therefore you must seek and find Me, that you may know and become I AM . . for only by entering in and being Me, can you come into the Consciousness of the Father, Who is One with Me."

**Remain faithful to the knowledge that your consciousness,** your I AMness, your awareness of being aware of the only reality. It is the rock on which all phenomena can be explained. There is no explanation outside of that. I know of no clear conception of the origin of phenomena save that consciousness is all and all is consciousness. That which you seek is already housed within you. Were it not now within you eternity could not evolve it. No time stretch would be long enough to evolve what is not potentially involved in you. You simply let it into being by assuming that it is already visible in your world, and remaining faithful to your assumption. it will harden into fact. Your Father has unnumbered ways of revealing your assumption. Fix this in your mind and always remember, "An assumption, though false, if sustained will harden into fact."

**"I AM a center in the Divine Mind,** a point of God-conscious life, truth and action. My affairs are divinely guided and guarded into right action, into correct results. Everything I do, say or think, is stimulated by the Truth. There is power in this word that I speak, because it is of the Truth and it is the Truth. There is perfect and continuous right action in my life and my affairs. All belief in wrong action is dispelled and made negative. Right action alone has power and right action is power, and Power is God . . . the Living Spirit Almighty.

This Spirit animates everything that I do, say or think. Ideas come to me daily and these ideas are divine ideas. They direct me and sustain me without effort. I AM continuously directed. I AM compelled to do the right thing at the right time, to say the right word at the right time, to follow the right course at all times. "All suggestion of age, poverty, limitation or unhappiness is uprooted from my mind and cannot gain entrance to my thought. I AM happy, well and filled with perfect Life. I live in the Spirit of Truth and am conscious that the Spirit of Truth lives in me. My word is the law unto its own manifestation, and will bring to me or cause me to be brought to its fulfillment. There is no unbelief, no doubt, no uncertainty. I know and I know that I know. Let every thought of doubt vanish from my mind that I may know the Truth and the Truth may make me free."

**I want to make the "I AM" very plain** so that whenever you speak these mystical words, you will do so with understanding. The "I AM" is the end of man's spiritual search. If man thinks that the "I AM" is the personal self he is in error and will receive negative results. However, when he realizes that the "I AM" is the Impersonal Self of All and in All, he is rewarded by positive results.

**I AM becoming a part of all that which I love.** All that
which I love is becoming a part of me. This is the creation
which is now achieving me. By this grace I AM ensouling all
that I love in the heavens of myself. Therefore, I AM love . .
love, the spirit and substance of me . . love, the thought and
life of me . . love, the body and being of me. In love I live,
move and have my being. I AM love and there is nothing else.
The substance of the universe is Love. Love is the inmost of
creation. Love is the soul of each atom. Love is the soul of the
air, and in each breath I breathe but love. There is nothing
but love, and what seems other is some lack of full welcome
to the Divine Reality.

Therefore, I AM Love: for love fashioned me and keeps my
sun of being ashine within me. Love loves through me and I
have no life but the life of love. Love loves in me. Love lives in
me. Love beings in me. All this dwelling together in unity,
which is the reality of me, is the magic grace of Love, ceasing
never for a breath, pausing never for a pulse thrill.

I AM a psalm of Love's Soul, never dying away into silence,
never discording with any hate, never blanking in any
voiceless and beingless world. Therefore, my whole business
is to love and take no thought of anxious care beyond loving.
My whole being is love. There is nothing but just Love. There
is nothing for me but just being what I AM. I AM Love. Love
is Endless Being.

**All that you formerly believed, you no longer believe.** You know now that there is no power outside of your own consciousness, your I AMness. Therefore you cannot turn to anyone outside of self. You have no ears for the suggestion that something else has power in it. You know the only reality is I AM, and I AM is your own consciousness, your I AMness. There is no other God. Therefore on this rock you build the everlasting church and boldly assume you are this Divine Being, self-begotten because you dared to appropriate that which was not given to you in your cradle, a concept of Self not formed in your mother's womb, a concept of self conceived outside of the offices of man.

**When you find yourself saying** . . "I AM tired," or "I AM sick," deny it at once. Say, instead . . NO! I AM is the name given to the God in me. I AM strong, active, refreshed. I AM energy, I AM strength, I AM power. I AM one with God. His strong, free, pure life is now active in and through every cell in my body. I AM one with all the good in the universe."

When you unify the rate of motion of your body with all that is good in the universe, you attract that good to you . . health, happiness, riches, love. But be sure to leave no obstructions between you and that good. Put no circuit breakers of hatred or resentment, no insulation of jealousy or envy, in its path. Say frequently . . "Dear Father, now I AM one with all the good in the universe. I freely forgive any who have ever seemed to harm me, and I ask forgiveness of all I may have seemed to harm."

Love attracts. Fear repels. Love draws the good to you. Fear acts as insulation that keeps all the good away from you.

**To him that hath (the consciousness of I AM)** shall be given; to him that hath not shall be taken away even that which he hath. It is one thing to say that we believe in God and quite another to be conscious of God. When we speak of the Universal Mind, we mean the Omnipresent Consciousness of God, the One Mind which inheres in all things, whose activity is Universal. Omnipresence completely fills the Universe. Everything is filled with the Principle of Life. Since His consciousness is our consciousness, we lack nothing. Mind is everywhere; there is no place where God is not. Man is a conscious, willing, thinking, knowing center of the Universal Mind of God. The I AM reacts to him according to the sum total of his beliefs. Man is Universal on the subjective side of life, and individual at the point of conscious perception. The individual uses the creative power of the Universal Mind every time he uses his own mind.

**God ("I AM") will manifest Himself** as you make a channel or mold for the manifestation. The little word "as" is very important, for it decides what the manifestation shall be. The Energy flowing through you now is God, but "it" manifests itself "as" you desire. "Whatsoever things ye desire, when ye pray, believe." The flowing iron will not change in Substance, but in form, "as" it passes through the mold. A pipe mold will be used if an iron pipe is desired, a valve mold for a valve, and a wheel mold for a wheel. "As you desire" is the mold which determines the form of manifestation of God. Meditate long over the following: "I AM the open channel through which the current of God is now flowing 'as' Health, Intelligence and Supply." Pause after Health . . Intelligence and Supply, so that you may have time to gain a clear realization of each.

**The real purpose, however, of these journeys** to the within, should be the change of thought, and for that reason should be taken whenever the need of mental change is felt. To begin, realize that the larger life within is the fullness of life, and cannot in any way lack the real essentials of life. Realize that the worlds within are ideal worlds, and are therefore not imperfect in any way. Realize that the new inner states of consciousness that you may discern, contain the unlimited possibilities of absolute existence, and are therefore neither incomplete nor imperfect in any way whatever.

Then realize that those inner places are not separated from you, but are necessary parts of your whole being, and also that the I AM, the real you, is at the very center of this whole being; and lastly, realize that whenever you turn your attention upon the potential, the within, the ideal, you are looking upon something that contains within itself all the elements of absolute perfection.

**Perhaps you have said "I AM" very often,** not perceiving its majesty, its mightiness, its tremendous force and power. When you realize that I AM is the name of God: "I AM is My name through all time. Go and tell my people that I AM has sent Me." I AM the Life. Can you make a concept of that? No! There can be no concept of that. There is only knowing, that I AM, always have been and always will be, the completeness of the Divine Spirit in man. I alone live in man, I created man and I live in man. I AM Life. There is no concept, but a knowing, an awareness.

**To the beginner in metaphysics and psychology** the statement that the real man is well may appear to be without foundation, but it is a statement that can be readily demonstrated in a number of ways. It can be demonstrated by pure reason, psychological research, finer personal experience, the evidence of higher states of consciousness, and several other effective methods. Besides, it is a truth that has been proclaimed in every age by the highest and best minds that the race has produced. The recognized foundation of this idea is found in the great truth that the real man, the spiritual man, the soul, the individuality, the "I AM," is created in the likeness of the Infinite; and as the Infinite of necessity always is well, the real man, created in the Divine Likeness, must also be well.

Those, however, who do not accept the statement that man is created in the image of God, and who claim that we have no scientific evidence for the belief that the human individuality is always well, are requested to examine carefully that something in man that we speak of as the conscious "I AM." If the conscious "I AM" were ever sick the very principle of human individuality would cease to be a principle, and, therefore, could not continue to maintain individuality. In other words, if that principle were sick, it would be out of harmony with natural law, and, therefore, would necessarily cease to be that factor that governs, controls and maintains conscious existence in man.

Accordingly the human entity would literally go to pieces and all the elements and the forces of the human system would be in chaos. The fact, however, that individuality persists in sickness as well as in health proves that the individuality itself is always well, must necessarily be always well.

**Mind is everywhere, in everything and through everything:** everything can respond to our thought. Jesus revealed this Truth when He spoke to the fig tree, saying, Bear no more fruit, henceforth; when He spoke to the winds and commanded them to be peaceful. When a unity has been established between the individual and the Universal I AM, Mind Substance can be directed into any channel.

The Universal Mind is always impersonal. It never decides who shall use it. It becomes personal only as It expresses through us. It doesn't matter who we are, or what we are. The sun shines on the good and the evil, and the rain falls on the just and the unjust. God is accessible and responsive to all. Cast thy bread upon the waters, for thou shalt find it after many days. The Law is exact. Thoughts are things, and things are thoughts. Cast your thought into the Universal Mind, and in due time it will return as form.

**When man discovers his I AM consciousness** to be the impersonal power of expression, which power eternally personifies itself in his conceptions of himself, he will assume and appropriate that state of consciousness which he desires to express; in so doing he will become that state in expression. "Ye shall decree a thing and it shall come to pass" can now be told in this manner: You shall become conscious of being or possessing a thing and you shall express or possess that which you are conscious of being.

The law of consciousness is the only law of expression. "I AM the way". "I AM the resurrection". Consciousness is the way as well as the power which resurrects and expresses all that man will ever be conscious of being.

**If we have clearly grasped the fact of our identity** with Universal Spirit, we shall find that, in the right direction, there is really no such thing as submission. Submission is to the power of another . . a man cannot be said to submit to himself. When the "I AM" in us recognizes a greater degree of I AMness . . if I may coin the word . . than it has hitherto attained, then, by the very force of this recognition, it becomes what it sees, and therefore naturally puts off from itself whatever would limit its expression of its own completeness.

**"To him that overcometh" . . that is, to him who recognizes** that already the world is overcome by the I AM, that there is nothing in all the universe but the I AM . . "will I give to eat of the hidden manna, and will give him a white stone, and on that stone a new name which no man knoweth, saving him who receives it."

**"All is within. Pray to your Father within."**

**If we do this,** . . knowing and believing that we, as Life, Intelligence, Truth and Substance are God, we cannot possibly manifest pain and disease, the opposite of God. Therefore, if we will meditate and think of the Father within, the I AM, the God Principle, Power and Life, which we the Thinker really are, we can experience only health and happiness.

**It is our conception of ourselves which frees** or constrains us, though it may use material agencies to achieve its purpose. Because life molds the outer world to reflect the inner arrangement of our minds, there is no way of bringing about the outer perfection we seek other than by the transformation of ourselves. No help cometh from without: the hills to which we lift our eyes are those of an inner range.

It is thus to our own consciousness that we must turn, our own I AM, as to the only reality, the only foundation on which all phenomena can be explained. We can rely absolutely on the justice of this law to give us only that which is of the nature of ourselves.

To attempt to change the world before we change our concept of ourselves is to struggle against the nature of things. There can be no outer change until there is first an inner change.

To attempt to change the world before we change our concept of ourselves is to struggle against the nature of things. There can be no outer change until there is first an inner change. As within, so without.

I AM not advocating philosophical indifference when I suggest that we should imagine ourselves as already that which we want to be, living in a mental atmosphere of greatness, rather than using physical means and arguments to bring about the desired changes.

Everything we do, unaccompanied by a change of consciousness, is but futile readjustment of surfaces. However we toil or struggle, we can receive no more than our concepts of Self affirm. To protest against anything which happens to us is to protest against the law of our being and our ruler ship over our own destiny.

**Before the world was "I AM";** before Abraham was "I AM"; when all things cease to be "I AM." I AM . . the only living Reality, . . the timeless One within man, . . "the lost Word" has been found. You have truly finished the work here when you have discovered who you are and return to the Glory of the Father. In the instant you become one with the All you find you are the world, and motion, gravitation, time and space are all within you. You know now that you are Alpha and Omega, that which was, is, and ever shall be. All things in space now revolve and dance as countless wheels within you, . . the Eternal wheel of the Law. You are the Creator of Heaven and earth whose dream is creation. You are also the dream, and when the dreamer awakens, the creation disintegrates, . . "When all things cease to be "I AM." All the world is but an infinite dream of the Infinite One. When we come out of this meditative phase we find we have fallen. "Remember man from whence thou hast fallen and do the first works."

**The statement "I AM well" should be used constantly** in the deepest and most sincere attitude of realization in order to secure a basis for healthful thinking. To this statement should be added as many constructive statements as may be necessary to express the true, the perfect and the ideal in every part of human life. The principle is, to think constantly that you are well and never permit yourself to think anything to the contrary. You will thus give the power of thought the power to produce health, and such thought will permeate every part of your body with the very life of health. By giving expression to the idea of health in every mental state, and in every action of consciousness and feeling, you add health producing power to the power of thought.

**The image-and-likeness man pours into "mankind"** a perpetual stream of ideas that the individual man arranges as thoughts and forms as substance and life. While this evolutionary process is going on there seem to be two men, one ideal and spiritual and the other intellectual and material, which are united at the consummation, the ideal man, Christ. When the mind attains an understanding of certain creative facts, of man's creative powers, it has established a directive, intelligent center that harmonizes these two men (ideal and spiritual vs. intellectual and material). This directive center may be named the I AM. It is something more than the human I. Yet when this human I has made union with the image-and-likeness I, the true I AM comes into action, and this is the Christ Jesus, the Son of God, evolved and made visible in creation according to divine law.

**"Ye shall know the truth and the truth shall set you free".** The truth that sets man free is the knowledge that his I AM consciousness is the resurrection and the life, that his consciousness both resurrects and makes alive all that he is conscious of being. Apart from consciousness, there is neither resurrection nor life. When man gives up his belief in a God apart from himself and begins to recognize his awareness of being to be God, as did Jesus and the prophets, he will transform his world with the realization, "I and My Father are one", but "My Father is greater than I". He will know that his consciousness . . I AM . . is God and that which he is conscious of being is the Son bearing witness of God, the Father.

**The speed with which you make any demonstration** will depend entirely upon the clarity of your mental picture. You cannot believe you are going to receive anything until you understand definitely what it is that you are going to receive. You must see the picture that you are presenting to Universal Mind very clearly. Not until your picture is clear do you have a good model or mold. The more perfect your picture, the more perfect your manifestation. The I AM working through the imagination not only can create but can also control. Imagination is the permanizing force that takes an invisible idea and builds it into form. Jesus was able to explore every negative condition and image it into perfection. The Perfect Man is created in the image of the I AM; through Spiritual vision, you can restore your body to its spiritual purity and perfection. The Universal Mind gives back to you what you deeply impress upon it. In the Silence, you are working in a spiritual foundry in which Universal Substance takes definite shape. If you are careless in your model or pattern, your product will be imperfect.

**When we learn to vibrate with God,** we shall be conscious that we are one with our Supply. This change in our rate of vibration is gained through the "Silence. If a musical note is sounded gradually through the various octaves until it reaches a very high pitch, it cannot be heard. Remember the second lesson, wherein I stated that things become invisible by increasing the rate of vibration. The greatest forces are "silent" because of their high rate of vibration. When one is absolutely still and his mind is taken off of forms and he thinks of the "Allness of I AM"; "Allness of Invisibility"; "Allness of Spirit," he finds that he has met this unseen Power face to face, and is one with Him. It is at this point that he loses the sense of the personal and gains the Impersonal.

**When speaking of the soul we usually refer to it as something we possess** instead of that something which actually is the possessor. We generally say "I have a soul" though the correct statement is "I AM a soul." The cause of this mistake is found in the fact that the ordinary person is only conscious of the surface. To him the outer man is the only real man, because he is not conscious of the deeper and more permanent principles of his being. He, therefore, thinks of the objective person as the true self and refers to what is distinct from the person, as something that is possessed by the person; but when the mind begins to expand, and consciousness becomes aware of the deeper and finer things in life, the discovery is made that the outer mind is not the basic mind, and that the person is not the real self.

The first discovery that is made through this mental growth is, that there is a subconscious mind, and if no further step is taken the conclusion is formed that the subconscious is the soul. There are many scientific minds today who have discovered the subconscious and believe they have found the soul, but they are mistaken. The subconscious is only the inner side of the personal mind and is, therefore, not any more a part of the soul than the outer mind. To find the soul, therefore, we must go beyond the subconscious into that state of consciousness that deals exclusively with the real, the permanent, the perfect and the absolute.

**Within you is the I AM, the Infinite, Eternal One Being.**
Because of this, you are. Because of this, you may so attune
unto and blend with the Infinite Being as to be able to say, in
sincerity and in truth, for yourself, I AM. In the realization of
the I AM, all dark problems are solved in light as nights are
dissolved in days.

**"I AM now realizing myself as Mind,** the power which
creates by thought. My mind is creative under Mind's Laws."

**To practice any art you must keep coming back** again and
again to it. Come back constantly, thoughtfully, eagerly,
deliberately. So you must practice this art of creating.
Practice closing the doors to the outer. Practice opening the
doors of the mind to the Father-force, the Great Universal
Force. Practice knowing I AM. Establish yourself in your
mind. Practice looking for the Force, the creative Force.
Speak to it. Practice . . practice . . practice . . practice.

**The wealth consciousness never carries a thought** of "I
have not," or "I cannot." Instead it carries: "I have" . . "I AM."
This continual carrying of constructive thinking makes the
thought become, as it were, second nature, and you find no
time for the opposite.

**Every atom is intelligent, and every organ is a being of intelligence;** it should therefore be treated as such and spoken to as such. Do not think of the organs in your body as so many physical organs, but as so many minds, because that is what they really are. The idealist is right, though he does not always make himself clear. Reduce anything to its last analysis, and you will find it to be MIND. Even iron, when reduced to its last analysis, becomes a MENTAL FORCE in nature; and many scientists believe if they could reduce still further they would find it to be absolute spirit.

What we speak of as matter is simply mind vibrating in the scale of tangibility. Matter does exist, but it does not exist apart from mind. Matter is mind in tangible expression. It is therefore strictly scientific to think of the body as visible mind, and to think of all the organs in the body as being centers of intelligence. And we shall find that when we take this view of the body, the physical system will no longer be a chunk of clay, but will become a more and more highly organized instrument, responding perfectly to every desire of the ruling mind the conscious mind, the "I AM" in man.

**Imagination is the only redemptive power in the universe.** However, your nature is such that it is optional to you whether you remain in your present concept of yourself . . a hungry being longing for freedom, health, and security . . or choose to become the instrument of your own redemption, imagining yourself as that which you want to be . . I AMness . ., and thereby satisfying your hunger and redeeming yourself.

**NEVER tell people about the fine thing you are going to do,** but wait until you have done it, and then show them the completed article. Never point to an empty lot and say: "I AM going to build a tower there"; but wait until the edifice is complete, and then if you like, say: "Look at the tower I *have* built." But when the tower is there it will not really be necessary to say anything at all, because it will speak for itself.

Talking about your plans before they have actually materialized, is the surest way to destroy them. It is a universal law of nature that the unborn child is protected from all contact with the world; in fact this is the real function of motherhood. Now the inspiration that comes to you is your child; you are its mother; and nature intends that you should protect and nourish that idea in secrecy and shelter, up to the moment when it is ready to emerge upon the material plane.

To chatter or boast about it is to expose it to the world and kill it. This applies to any new enterprise that you may be contemplating, as well as to a new idea. An important business deal, for instance, a large sale, the buying of a house, the forming of a partnership, should be protected in the same way. Don't discuss these things at the luncheon table, or anywhere else.

Keep your business to yourself. Of course it is quite permissible to consult experts, and to reveal your plan where it is absolutely necessary to do so. This is nourishing the idea, not exposing It. It is chatter, gossip, and boasting that are to be avoided. In quietness and confidence shall be your strength.

**As we vibrate (think) in the Universal Mind,** we have the consciousness of unity. The stronger our consciousness the more we are able to receive. A simple illustration will make this point clear. A piece of ice is placed in a glass of water. The atoms of ice, as we know, are vibrating at a low rate; the atoms of water are vibrating at a higher rate. If the ice is allowed to remain in the water long enough it will melt, and after a time it will be water. The ice disappears (as ice) and is changed back to water because the rate of its vibration is increased. All the atoms in the glass then vibrate at the same rate. Vibration is at the base of all form; it is independent of physical force. When we learn how to vibrate consciously in the Universal Mind, we shall know that we are one with the substance of I AM. The highest vibrations and the greatest power are silent. When we enter the Silence, we change our rate of vibration from the slow and negative to the fast and positive. We lose our sense of the personal as we merge with the impersonal I AM.

**"I AM the Lord who heals you" is our guarantee** of healing and our proof that we must credit all healing, by any means whatever, to I AM. "He" alone is life, and is the Source of all the energies of life expressing themselves in material form. In the vegetable world "He gives their fruit for meat, and their leaves for medicine." Life, sense and intelligence exist in all living things, because I AM is in all living things. Therefore God, who is all that really is, is the I AM That I AM, with whom any intelligence, in conscious union, may say, "I AM."

**It is said that most of Mind (nine-tenths),** like the iceberg, is submerged. Just because you cannot see yourself does not mean that you do not exist. An iceberg is often seen floating against the current. This is explained by what I have just said . . that it is nine-tenths submerged. One-tenth is seen in the current flowing north but it is buried so far down that nine-tenths of it is in another current going in the opposite direction. Many people are able to go against the current of events, and succeed. They are called the strong souls. They are strong, however, because they understand that they are not the visible man but the invisible "I AM."

**Because consciousness is the only reality** I must assume that I AM already that which I desire to be. If I do not believe that I AM already what I want to be, then I remain as I AM and die in this limitation. Man is always looking for some prop on which to lean. He is always looking for some excuse to justify failure. This revelation gives man no excuse for failure. His concept of himself is the cause of all the circumstances of his life. All changes must first come from within himself; and if he does not change on the outside it is because he has not changed within.

**In Mental Science, the great principle laid down is this:**
Man is conjoined to the Eternal Life Principle. He is that
Principle . . its very self in objectivity . . and in proportion as
he becomes intellectually conscious of this tremendous
truth, he finds an unfailing supply to all his needs, and
grows more into a knowledge of his own mastery.

We are manifestations of the unchanging Life Principle; of
the Universal Spirit of Being; the inextinguishable I AM. It is
the soul to nature . . the body. It is internal man. Man is the
external of it. And the seeming two are one.

This Law, or Principle, is man in subjectivity.

Visible man is the Law, or Principle, in objectivity.

When the race knows this great truth, it will appreciate its
own dignity and worth and power, and then there will be no
more (so-called) sin and sickness and death; no more
shedding of tears; no more want or sorrow or the feebleness
of old age. We shall know that we are one with the deathless
Law of Being, and that our progression through the realms of
the universe will be by constantly knowing more and more of
the power and beauty and opulence of the Law, which is the
vital spark within us.

**You are conscious of yourself . . self-conscious** . . because
you are reacting to things external to yourself. They exist to
you and are held as concepts in your mind, and this gives
you a feeling of separation. Without a feeling of separation
you could have no knowledge of unity, and without knowing
imperfection you could have no knowledge of perfection. But
the Perfection of Reality cannot be perceived by man's mind,
for when you perceive something you have perceived what it
is. You cannot perceive the Reality because it is beyond your
perception. What we perceive in our imagination is not
Perfection of Reality, only an idea of it; but to know that It is,
is self satisfying and complete. It is . . I AM That I AM. "I and
the Father are one."

**The I AM in us is the only God we shall ever know.** If we
recognize It and accept It as health, It will manifest as an
abundant health. If we recognize It and accept It as
happiness, It will manifest as abundant happiness. If we
recognize It and accept It as opulence, It will manifest as
abundant prosperity. As we release this Divine Energy, It will
become to us anything we believe It to be. Since we actually
live and move in this Energy, there can be no thought of
bringing God down to us from some high place in the sky,
but rather of lifting our thought to the heavenly place in our
own minds in which we may more fully comprehend Him. In
the Silence, we cultivate a deep consciousness of unity with
the Universal Creative Mind. We merge with It until It
becomes our own Consciousness. We take from It as much
as we are prepared to receive.

**Go to sleep with the purpose of going into the subconscious** and doing something there that is constructive, upbuilding and wholesome; but as you entertain such intentions, place your mind in an attitude that is perfectly serene. We should approach all work in the serene attitude, whether we are to act objectively or subjectively. Perfect rest for any part of the system during the waking state can be secured by learning to withdraw consciousness absolutely from one part and causing it to act wholly upon another part. Consciousness is the result of the "I AM" expressing life, thought and being, and therefore consciousness acts on a certain plane, or in a certain part, so long as the I AM gives expression to itself upon that plane, or in that part.

Consciousness is always active. An inactive consciousness is as impossible as a dark ray of light. When anything is conscious, it must do something, and it continues to do something, either objectively or subjectively, so long as conscious existence continues. Since consciousness means action in every instance, it is evident that no part of the system can rest until we become unconscious of that part. So long as we are conscious of that part, we will act upon that part, and the energy in that particular place will continue to be used.

**Say to yourself till you feel and believe it,** "Mind is the One Creative Power, and I AM That Mind. All the potentialities of creativeness are existent within me at this very moment. I AM a part of the One Creativeness and my mind, when I so realize and use it, acts under its own creative law and is in a limitless degree productive."

**WHAT is that which makes you different from any other person?** It is the degree of God you are expressing. All life and form is a variation of motion or vibration, and in the degree that you are living and vibrating, or radiating the Universal Substance, in that degree you are YOU . . the I AM . . the manifestation of God-Power. This Substance fills all space, and is as free as the air we breathe. It permeates our systems. We can shut it out of our lives, as we can air and sunshine, which are universal agents, or we can open body, mind and spirit to the influx of this Divine Radiance, vibrating it through our beings, and radiating it with soul-force to others, who are not yet able to make themselves receptive to its power.

You are YOU in the measure that you appropriate and use and vibrate to this Universal Intelligence. I AM ALL THAT I REALIZE OF THIS DIVINE LIFE AND SUBSTANCE, and YOU ARE ALL THAT YOU REALIZE OF THIS DIVINE POWER; but through divine Love, continually opening up our spiritual vision, as we reach out for Truth and Wisdom, we can realize more and more of the God-nature . . the I AM . . and, realizing more, a wider and wider vision of love and service opens up to us, and we will express more and become more like Divinity. Daily affirming: I AM LOVE, I AM HEALTH, I AM WISDOM, I AM POWER, attracts to us the divine Substance enfolding the universe, and we expand in mental and spiritual consciousness from the DIVINE IMAGE into Divine Reality.

**There is no reality in the world other than your consciousness** . . your I AMness. Although you may now seem to be what you do not want to be, all you need do to change it, and to prove the change by circumstances in your world, is to quietly assume that you are that which you now want to be, and in a way you do not know you will become it. There is no other way to change this world. "I AM the way." My I AMness, my consciousness is the way by which I change my world.

**If you are thinking the material thought, which means** . . if you are thinking of the thing you want . . your mental vibrations are too low, as they register but 40%. The more you realize the Spirit of the thing or the Substance of the thing, the higher your mental vibrations. When you are thinking of I AM and knowing that I AM is the Substance (Spirit) of every form, your vibrations may even attain the one hundred percent rate, which is perfect Realization.

**The universal Substance with which you are working in** the Silence is the most sensitive Substance in the world. In its native state, it is unformed, but It solidifies or assume any form possible to your belief. It distributes Itself through the visual power of your mind. The I AM sends its Substance into the picture that the directive power of yours will give. You use your will to train the imagination to see only those things which you wish to experience. The quickest way to blot out an adverse or disastrous thought is to ask yourself this question: Is this what I want to happen?

**When sickness appears in the body affirm, "I AM well,"** and know that it is the truth, because you, the real you, the individuality, the real "I AM," always is well. As you affirm this statement think of the absolute wholeness that permeates your being, and keep the mental eye single upon this absolutely perfect state. In this way perfect health becomes your ideal, and all your thinking will become healthful.

Every thought you think will accordingly contain the power of health, and as your thought is so will also be the states and conditions of your personality. The statement, "I AM well," however, should not simply be used when sickness appears in the body. It is a statement that every mind should think at all times, because it is the truth about the true being; and the person who always thinks the truth about the true being, will always be as well in body and mind as he is in the perfections of his true being. Live and think constantly the statement, "I AM well" and you always will be well.

**When you know that consciousness (I AM)** is the one and only reality . . conceiving itself to be something good, bad or indifferent, and becoming that which it conceived itself to be . . you are free from the tyranny of second causes, free from the belief that there are causes outside of your own mind that can affect your life. In the state of consciousness of the individual is found the explanation of the phenomena of life.

**Be ye transformed by the renewing of your mind.** The Truth can only be known as the entire consciousness is surrendered to the Universal Mind which is Oneness, Wholeness and Completeness. The Law must be fulfilled in our consciousness by the clear perception that I AM is all. Merely thinking the Truth never changes anyone. It is the conscious knowing of the Truth that changes man from a material to a spiritual basis. Knowing the Truth means to have the true idea of Principle or God and the true idea of man. The word Principle used so frequently in our lessons means the Law of the I AM, Universal Mind, Spiritual Substance, the Omnipresent, Omnipotence and Omniscience of our own Minds. One cannot think of the word Principle without losing the thought of the personal. Since the true nature of God is impersonal, the word will gradually clear the concept of a personal God subject to all the limitations which personality connotes.

**How would you conduct yourself** if you fully realized your oneness with I AM, if you could truly believe that He is constantly offering you life, love and every good thing your heart can desire? Well, that is exactly what He is doing! So act as if you already had the thing you want. Visualize it as yours. See the picture clearly in every detail in your mind's eye. Then LET I AM make it manifest. Do what you can, of course, with what you have, where you are, but put your dependence upon I AM, and LET His good gifts come to you.

**Let us think together now for our bodies.** Let u go within the chamber of mind. Let us close our eyes and let us think . . I AM creative through my thinking, for what I think I attract. I AM turning to the force of I AM for my help. I, looking toward this presence of Force, am thinking PERFECT BODY. As I think perfect body, I speak lovingly to the Force. Our Force that is within us, holy and sacred is Thy nature. Come forth now in my body as I AM thinking PERFECT BODY. Come forth as perfection.

**Now pause for a few moments and think** over this wonderful fact . . All the Energy in the Universe is "I AM"; all the "I AM" in the Universe is Success. It was Moses who realized his oneness with this power when, as stated in the third chapter of Exodus, he became fully conscious of . . "I AM" That "I AM." "I AM" is impersonal and since Man is that "I AM," Man is impersonal and is always one with this omnipotent, omnipresent, omniscient Power.

**"You did not choose me, I have chosen you."** My concept of myself molds a world in harmony with itself and draws men to tell me constantly by their behavior who I AM.

**But how, you may ask, can I convince my Higher Self that** I have riches or any other good thing, when my common sense tells me that I am in debt up to my ears and creditors are hounding me day and night?

You can't . . if you keep thinking and acting DEBTS. But here is a psychological fact: The Higher Self accepts as fact anything that is repeated to it in convincing tones often enough. And once it has accepted any statement as fact, it proceeds to do everything possible to MAKE IT TRUE!

That is the whole purpose of affirmations . . to bring the I AM in You to accept as true the conditions that you desire, to the end that He will then proceed to bring them into being. It is a sort of autosuggestion. You keep saying to yourself that you ARE rich, that you HAVE the things you desire, until the constant repetition is accepted by the Higher Self and translated into its physical equivalent.

Debts? Don't worry about them. Remember that the shadow of growing grain kills the weeds. Keep your mind on the good you want and it will kill off the evil you fear, just as the turning on of light dispels darkness. A farmer does not have to hoe the weeds out of growing wheat, any more than you have to sweep the darkness out of a room. Neither do you have to worry about debts or lack. Put all your thoughts and all your faith in the riches you are praying for (you feel you already have), and let them dispel the debts.

But don't worry if you can't summon such faith right out of the blue. Most of us have to lead up to it gradually. Start with Coue's well-known affirmation . . "Every day in every way we are getting richer and richer." Use that to prepare your Higher Self for the stronger affirmations. Then, when your faith has grown stronger, claim the thing you want!

Affirm that you HAVE it . . and insofar as possible, ACT AS THOUGH YOU HAD IT!

Write it in your heart that each day is the best day of the year, that NOW is the accepted time, NOW is the day of salvation. Then thank God for the good you have been praying for, believe that you HAVE received and give thanks.

Remember this: I AM, God's will always works when you offer no resistance to it. So pray . . and then LET His good come to you. Don't fight the conditions about you. Don't try to overcome the obstacles in your path. BLESS them . . know that I AM is in them . . that if you will LET them, they will work WITH you for good. Have faith not only in God, but in people and things. Don't look for a miracle to happen. Don't expect an angel from Heaven to come and open the way. Know that God works through ordinary people and things, and it is through them that your good will come.

So bless THEM. Serve them as you would the Lord, doing each thing that is given you to do as though you were the greatest genius. And all day long, as the thought occurs to you, keep repeating to yourself . . "Every day in every way I AM getting richer and richer," or whatever it is that you desire.

**You walk in the consciousness, your own I AMness,** of being that which you want to be, no one sees it as yet, but you do not need a man to roll away the problems and the obstacles of life in order to express that which you are conscious of being.

**He that losses his life shall find it in the Universal Source.** The only thing that can be lost (set aside) are the false belief of the limited personal self. Divine Substance and Power cannot function in a divided or personal consciousness. The mind must be One and the attitude impersonal before we can experience the Power. Greater is he that is in you than he that is in the world. The Impersonal Life is the I AM or spiritual consciousness, which says, If any man will come after me, let him deny himself and take up his cross daily. The cross represents the Universal Mind of God through which the false beliefs of personal consciousness are denied or set aside by the God Consciousness. By lifting one's thought to the Universal Mind, one crosses out all that is opposed to or at variance with God.

**A sick body is made so by destructive thoughts and emotions.**

Think in this manner . . I, the free, divine thinker that I AM . . I, looking at my body and seeing the damage that has been done, can repair, remake, rebuild if I refuse to indulge in the thoughts and emotions which have caused the damage and reverse the order of my thinking and feeling. I AM creative in my power to think for always I can draw into my thinking the force which is about and in and through me. Have faith in this truth, trust in it, practice it. Success depends upon using this creative law. Now create the perfect body idea. Forget the criticisms, fears, resentments, discouragements and heartaches.

**There is one point I desire to impress upon the mentality**
ere we go further: It is very natural, when first entering the
silence to mentally criticize the progress of others . . to
imagine we are greater or have gone higher than the "other
fellow." Comparisons are unworthy of the thought, and are
classed in the not "I" series and indicate a lack of
development. Simply ignore all consideration of others and
realize the fact that "I" AM Wisdom. "I" AM Knowledge. "I" AM
Power. "I" AM Divine. "I" am a center around which all else
must circle.

In just the degree that the pupil realizes he is a center will he
be able to manifest its drawing power, which awakens in the
soul a desire to scale the summit and plant Truth's banner
on the heights. Let the pupil realize from the center of his
being comes the great power of concentration, which is the
first step on the road to realization, and in order to
concentrate, the pupil must compel himself to pay attention.
Attention is concentration. No one ever concentrated who
said, "I AM going to concentrate." Forget what you are going
to do and the thing is done.

**Through the imagining power of Divine Mind,** Spirit propels Itself into creation. Will power is never creative; to suppose that God had to will things into being would be to suppose an opposite or contending force to God. The Substance that you have extracted from your original and associated ideas must now be reproduced in form. It must be translated from the invisible into the visible. It must be materialized so that you can possess it in a tangible way. Each step brings you nearer to the object of your desire. The Universal Substance that you are causing to stand around you idea, whose center is I AM, is permeable, impressible, plastic, retentive and sensitive. The I AM, or Spirit, will vitalize any picture that you visualize. It will draw from the Universal Substance whatever is necessary for its material fulfillment.

**I AM truth, and living is but my growing conscious** of myself. With what torch of truth I discover the universe I discover myself. I cannot go beyond what I AM. The universe cannot speak but in my own language. Only as it is native to me are its meanings wisdom and power within me. What truth I AM, that truth is God to me.

**Man should affirm to himself "I AM not passing with time,** because time does not pass; time is. I AM living in the now, and the now continues eternally to be the now. I AM living and growing now, but I AM not passing towards age. There is no age, and I do not pass; I AM." When man develops the "I AM" consciousness, he will attain the realization of what he is now; he will discern that his present nature is limitless in possibility, and that the conscious possession of more and more of the richness of his nature will come, not from more and more years of development, but from more and more present realization. He will discern that he may accomplish whatever he has in mind by perpetually increasing his present realization of what is latent in his nature now. He will not look to the future for greater attainments, but to the growth of the present, and will consequently concentrate the whole of attention upon the now. To live in the realization of the now, with no direct thought of the past or the future, is to eliminate from mind the "passing of time" attitude; and when this attitude is removed the consciousness of age will disappear completely.

**"I AM the door"... all that ever came before me are thieves and robbers"** shows me that my consciousness is the one and only entrance into the world of expression; that by assuming the consciousness of being or possessing the thing which I desire to be or possess is the only way by which I can become it or possess it; that any attempt to express this desirable state in ways other than by assuming the consciousness of being or possessing it, is to be robbed of the joy of expression and possession.

**And if you want to know the Lost Word of Power** . . the secret name of God . . it is "I AM ". "Before Abraham," said Jesus, "was I AM." And throughout the Old Testament, you find frequent references to God as the eternal I AM.

That is the secret of success in all prayer, in everything you do . . that there is only one present, only one bit of time you need to worry about . . the everlasting NOW. Whatsoever things ye ask for when ye pray, believe that ye RECEIVE them." Not, mind you, that you are going to get them in some dim and distant future, but that you HAVE them now!

You are part of the great I AM. You HAVE everything of good now. You ARE perfect. You HAVE health and strength and power and riches and happiness. It remains only for you to make this manifest. How are you to do this?

1 — By sowing your seeds of the harvest you wish to reap. (Claiming your desire is a present reality)

2 — By cultivating it through serenity and faith.

3 — By visualization . . seeing in your mind's eye the abundant harvest you are praying for.

4 — By thanking I AM for it.

**As I ascend in consciousness the power and the glory** that was mine return to me and I too will say "I have finished the work thou gavest me to do." The work is to return from my descent in consciousness, from the level wherein I believed that I was a son of man, to the sphere where I know that I AM one with my Father and my Father is God.

**Any attempt to move anything out of the body or the circumstances,** anything which does not have a cause in Divine Mind, will nullify the demonstration. Disagreeable conditions have no existence whatever outside of consciousness; therefore we must look to our own thoughts for a solution of our problems. The human body and the body of one's affairs will automatically express the prevailing state of thought in the mind. When we discover that our Mind is the Mind of God, that His Power is our Power, we shall be so close to Him that He will be in everything we do. When the I AM is given dominion over our consciousness, it works perfectly. Realizing this, we can walk perfectly, hear perfectly and see perfectly. Let this mind be in you.

**To begin the day with the statement, "I AM young,**
because my entire being is perpetually renewed," is to place
the strong, clear thought of the morning in perfect harmony
with the natural process of perpetual renewal, and every
state of the mind that is formed during the day will be a
youth producing state. It is well, however, to frequently
repeat this statement during the day, though these
repetitions should never have the slightest trace of the
mechanical. When you affirm, in thought, "I AM young,"
make that affirmation so clear, so positive and so strong that
you can feel the vibrations of youth and vigor thrill every
atom in your being; and try to feel these vibrations so deeply
that their actions will penetrate into the very depth of the
subconscious.

To train the mind to think the truth about the renewing
process that is ever keeping the body young, it is highly
important to affirm the statement: "My entire being is ever
young and new, because nature permits no cell to remain in
my body more than a few months, when it builds a new one
in its place." To this may be added, "Nature gives me a new
body every year"; "My mind is new every morning," and "My
life comes forth from the Creator of life every moment as
fresh and as new as the flowers of the springtime."

**I know I AM the creator of my own world, I AM the
center of my own world;** I AM the center round which my
world revolves and in that center is Reality. As soon as
Reality becomes known to the mind of the individual it
expresses itself. The mind becomes clear and Reality is
expressed outwardly . . then there is no longer any craving,
no longer any opposing images, there is only the direct
manifestation on the outer plane, that is the Christ.

**Remember, the I AM in you is your part of Divinity.** Some sage put it . . "Whatever the Creator is, I AM." How often have you said . . "I AM poor, I AM sick, I AM ignorant, I AM weak" . . and thus fastened these evils upon yourself? You acknowledged a lack of something. What can you build with minus quantities? Only emptiness, void.

Reverse all that. Whenever you say "I AM", whenever you thus call upon the God in You, make it something you WANT. "I AM rich. I AM powerful. I AM well and whole and strong. I AM happy. I AM perfect in every way."

Make an I AM Scrap Book, with your picture on the first page, then pictures of supermen or genii or whatever your idea of power may be scattered throughout the pages of the book. Put in it pictures of all the things you would like to be and do. And fill it with such affirmations as these:

"The Spirit of Prosperity fills my mind and overflows into my affairs. I AM is my perfect will; through me it is done." "There is only one Presence and one Power in my life . . I AM, the Good Omnipotent. I AM is my inexhaustible source of abundant supply. The riches of the Spirit now fill my mind and affairs. I think prosperity. I talk prosperity, and I know that prosperity and success are mine."

**Freedom is assured when we let go of the personal sense,** the consciousness of the body which we have so long separated from the Universal Mind of God. To tell a blind man that he can see, or a lame man that he can walk, is the truth of the Omnipresent Self. He may desire to know this, try to imagine or pray that it is so, but until he is conscious only of the I AM within him as the center of his sight or his walking, nothing will happen. When one is absolutely relaxed, conscious only of being conscious, when he has taken his attention away from himself and from his world and fixed his attention only upon the I AM within him, he will be in tune with everything in the Universe and have dominion over it.

**"All the Life, Strength and Vitality** that is in God, is now flowing into my body abundantly. I AM attuned to the Divine Energy of Divine Life, Light and Love." Use this daily, sincerely, and it will help you more than I can tell. You will realize its Truth more and more.

**I AM a creative being.** I create by thinking an idea, at the same time knowing that I AM connected with a universal force which carries out to fulfillment the idea I AM thinking. That makes me free for I can think what I wish to think.

**You will then have discovered through actual conscious** experience that individual existence is impossible without perpetual health, and also that that part of you which is life must therefore be perfectly well at all times. As you grow in the consciousness of your own individual "I AM," this truth will become clearer and clearer, until finally every thought you think will be actually permeated with the realization that the real man is well, and that you are the real man. Whether you are conscious or not of the fact that you are the soul, and that the soul or the real man is well, you can easily reason the matter out. Pure reason will convince you that there is something in man that is always well; and when you examine that something, you will find it to be your own individuality the self-conscious "I AM" the real you.

**We are Thinking Beings! I AM a Thinking Being!** You are a Thinking Being!

Through your thinking you create for there is a force, a mighty universal force, wise and loving, everywhere present, within and without. This universal force runs according to your thinking and produces the outer visible forms of your thinking. This force flows toward good or evil as you think. If you reverse your thinking, you reverse the flow of the force. You are creative then, for as you think so you become.

You are permitted to think anything you will. You, of all created beings have the power of choice. You need only think what you allow yourself to think. If you object to an idea, you can refuse to think that idea. Then that idea and that thing cannot be created in your world.

**"There are many people who are today convinced that there is a technique of creative thinking** and that when man uses his mind in this certain way, that he not only uses his own creative power at its highest potential, but that he predisposes both people and events to respond to his purposes. "Doubtless we are already obeying most of this mental technique, but to know its steps and consciously obey them, will certainly intensify our creative thinking and so hasten the result. Let me give you a brief statement of the exact nature of this creative technique. Here it is in a formula:

"When I AM conscious that my mind is an
Absolute creative power,
Whatever I ardently desire,
Vividly imagine,
Joyously believe is possible,
and Expectantly act toward,
Will Inevitably manifest.

**Don't let anything that has happened in your life discourage you.** Don't let poverty or lack of education or past failures hold you back. There is only one power . . the I AM in you . . and it can do anything. If in the past you have not used that power, that is too bad as far as the past is concerned, but it is not too late. You can start NOW. "Be still, and know that I AM God."

**The thought which we must keep in mind is that God Consciousness** does not change or add anything to us. Our only purpose is to reveal the Life Principle and Power of the Universal Mind, God. When we treat, or attempt to move negative conditions such as disease and poverty, we are recognizing two powers and binding the negative conditions to us. We are unconsciously admitting that the good we seek does not exist. Jesus said, I AM come not to destroy, but to fulfill. Even a thought about lack, or a desire to add substance to ourselves, is to discredit the Mind which is the Substance of all things. The positive qualities of the I AM will always become visible when we drop from our consciousness the belief in the negative qualities.

### ONENESS WITH THE UNIVERSAL POWER:

I know that Nature's modes are all conceived in abundance. With lavish hand she pours out her treasure from a limitless fountain of rich inner energies. I mentally put myself in tune with Mother Nature's abundance realizing that this is the mode of Infinite Mind. I, too, desire, think, feel and act with a sense of abundance and power. Since I AM a part of Mind, the One Creativeness, . . an individualization of this One Limitless Creativeness, why should I not pour out from the limitless reservoirs of inner power, not only abundance for myself but rich treasures for all those whom I know? I think of myself as a focal point for the limitless productiveness of the universe. Whatever I can think and believe, I can produce. This is the message of the universe to me. I believe it. I act upon it. It is done, or is even now being done.

**First of all, let us define Mind. Mind is thinking Substance** . . not the Substance by which we think, but Substance that thinks. It works by law and is omnipresent. Mind is something. There is more evidence of Mind than there is of matter. I AM in this thinking Substance called Mind and I cannot move any part of my body without moving it by and through this wonderful something. "This something" surrounds us. I AM walking through it, thinking into it and it thus registers the vibrations of every thought and word. As you think into this Substance, it is transformed; not changed, but transformed.

Remember, as you think so do you receive. If you think negatively you will receive negative results. When they come to you in the form of failure, sickness, trouble, disappointment and hatred, do not complain . . it is what you prayed for, for thought is prayer. Change your thinking . . your thoughts. People complain of their ill luck and do not seem to realize that they bring it upon themselves. They speak into this universal Substance and form it and it returns to them. "Ask and ye shall receive." Ask positively and ye shall receive positively. It is according to your word . . this you must realize.

**Here it is: "I have arisen; I have awakened.** I AM the Reality, Truth and Life. I will persevere in my endeavor and advancement until I have come into my own higher Self, which is boundless in capacity. I will remain steadfast in the Soul quest and Attainment.

If you will follow this simple mantra, its mystical effect will prove a God's truth to you. Can I make this statement stronger, and further convince you? Try it. Knowledge is the attribute of man. Wisdom is the attribute of the Infinite. Both knowledge and wisdom come to you from their source, the Absolute, whom we call God.

**I AM is the Omnipresent, Universal Mind of God.** It is the Principle of divine Unity underlying all creation; when Self-conscious in man. There is no separation in Spirit; the individual mind can never be separated from the Universal Mind.

**GOD, is your own consciousness, your I AM.** That is the only creative law in the world. Of what are you conscious of being? Although you cannot see your objective with the limited focus of your three-dimensional mind, you are now that which you have assumed you are. Walk in that assumption and remain faithful to it.

**Don't say . . "When this bill is paid** . . or this crisis past . . I shall feel so relieved." Instead, say . . "I AM relieved, I feel so content and peaceful now that this load is off my shoulders." How will you act when you get the thing you want? Well, act that way now, think that way . . and before you know it, you will BE that way.

**In the Silence, you step out of yourself and into God.** You reach the fullness of God, your unity with the Whole, through the realization that I AM, alone, speaks, thinks and acts. The more spiritual your growth, the greater your capability for perceiving the things of the spirit. The loftier your spiritual enlightenment, the finer and higher your perception until you come to realize, know and comprehend the ever-hovering Presence.

**These are the two names which give you dominion.** You have dominion if, as you walk the earth, you know that your consciousness, your I AMness is God, the one and only reality. You become aware of something you would like to express or possess. You have the ability to feel that you are and possess that which but a moment before was imaginary.

**"The sun shines on the good and the evil, and the rain falls on the just and the unjust."** It does not matter whether you are black or white, illiterate or educated, or which church you belong to . . the sun shines on all and the rain, when it falls, falls on all. So with Mind . . it is universal. We are all surrounded by the same thinking Substance. We are all immersed in the same Presence. Mind power is the cause of physical energy. Your physical energy depends not so much upon what you eat as upon what you are thinking. As you think, the very atoms begin to vibrate in the muscles; your nerves vibrate . . you vibrate and you move.

The old idea of the universe was that the Creator had made the universe like a watch, and after establishing it, had wound it up, put it into operation and had then gone away. The newer idea is that divine Wisdom and Intelligence are in the watch. Mind is everywhere. Everything thinks. That includes everything. You are in a thinking world; man has needed this knowledge . . that all is Mind and its infinite Manifestation. The universe is alive with this thinking Substance.

**All we shall ever want or ever possibly desire** is in the Invisible now. When you have (in your hand) the object which you have desired, do not say . . "Now I have it." You will never have it in your possession materially, until you realize that you have it in the Invisible first. I AM, God (Invisible Substance called Spirit) is the Giver and the Gift. It is not more things we want but more of the consciousness of the Substance (God . . underlying Principle) of the thing. I AM is Cause and Effect, so that it is all Cause, for I AM is All and in All.

**Know that your consciousness, your I AMness,** is the only reality. Then know what you want to be. Then assume the feeling of being that which you want to be, and remain faithful to your assumption, living and acting on your conviction. Always make it fit that pattern.

**In our study it is very important that we not only hold the fixed idea** . . "There is Plenty" but this advanced one . . "There is Plenty everywhere." The belief in space has been responsible for our belief in lack. The student understands now that if the subconscious mind believes in lack of any kind, such conditions of lack will be vibrated to the individual who entertains the thought.

Once more I offer scientific data showing conclusively that "lack" is not true. As the mind is convinced at first, intellectually, it accepts the Absolute more easily and without conscious resistance. The invisible Spirit Substance is found to be not only abundant, but everywhere. Of course since it is everywhere, lack can be nowhere.

Instead of believing in vacancies, we discover that the whole universe is filled with "that something" out of which everything comes and is made into form. Therefore there is no lack; no want; only in consciousness. There is not one place in the universe where there is lack. A hole in the ground is filled with "that something" which is invisible; which is intangible; "that something" out of which things are made . . therefore space does not exist.

**It is now easy to see that your desire in the without** must through "the silence," or in prayer be carried to the inner sanctuary of the soul ("thy closet") and there placed as a definite request before the Father . . the I AM. This is "asking." The Spirit asks, "What shall I do for thee?" You answer by naming your desire, . . by asking.

Lifted to the spiritual plane, your request is there quickened by the Spirit and becomes a conception in your soul. Now it is a conceived idea, . . a seed planted in the soil of your soul. As any other seed, it will germinate, develop first in the invisible, and in "fullness of time" come forth.

The mind, conscious of this, expects the fulfillment, as does a mother her child, or a farmer his harvest. This is "believing." It is "holding in mind" the form of the perfected expression. The mother believes she has her child, even when it is being formed in the invisible.

The farmer believes he has his harvest, even while it is growing beneath the soil. We must "believe we have" our demonstration while it is being formed for us in the inner realms of consciousness, for it is "believing we have" that holds definitely in mind the form of our desire, and gives it the desired form. When we believe we have, seeing in faith, "the invisible," we have.

In fullness of time, this thought form is delivered upon the physical plane. As a mother's birth effort delivers her child, so you through physical effort perfect your demonstration. It requires strength to speak and act in a way that is true to the conception, and to carry out the idea held in mind.

The idea of health and the thought form of health must not be denied by the action of sickness or by resorting to external means to try to get well. The *thought form* is perfect health now.

If the soul conception is abundance, the action must carry out that idea. The spirit of the action must conform to the image. Until abundance manifests the amount of expenditure need not be increased, but the spirit of the mind must be one of richness, and what is spent must be allowed to leave the hands cheerfully and willingly in no consciousness of loss or of self-denial, but rather in the attitude of trust and thanksgiving because of the ever present supply now being made manifest. Be true. Spirit, soul, mind and body must agree to bring forth even as you have conceived, exactly "according to your faith." "Ye shall reap in due time (the time of fulfillment) if ye faint not. "Be not faithless, but believing."

**One great difference between the subjective mind** and the subconscious mind is to be noted, namely, the subconscious mind creates and objectifies all that it believes; the subjective mind does not. Since the subconscious is the creative mind it begins to work out forms in the visible world, according to the patterns given it by the I AM Self.

If the subconscious mind received all the impressions of the objective mind and created them, what a confusion we would have! If all the false beliefs regarding sickness, and all the false ideas of lack were to be received in the subconscious mind, man would live in constant poverty while here and pass on not having learned the Truth.

**Word, thought, idea and Spirit-power bear exactly the same relation** to each other that the key, hammer, string and vibration bear to each other in a piano. The vibration, or power within the string is released as sound to the ear only as the key in connection with it is struck. The key C moves the hammer C which touches the string C and releases the vibration C. In no other way can that particular tone be brought forth. If we want the tone C, we must be particular to strike the key C. In the same way, the word health moves the thought health, and awakens the idea health until the vibration or feeling of health is released in consciousness.

It is for this reason that the weak are told to say "I AM strong." Strength is what the weak wish to experience, therefore they must say it and think it and in exact fulfillment of the law of faith they will feel it, but they will not do so as long as they persist in saying "weak."

These true words, or words declaring the truth of Being, are the "keys of the kingdom" to which Jesus referred when he told Peter, the man of faith, that they would be given to him. They are given to every faithful soul who will lift the consciousness above the testimony of the senses, or the opinions of others, and voice the Truth from the prompting of the Spirit within. In no other way can the "church" of Christ which is the "temple of the body" be built, for it must be formed from within, but can be only as the word which calls it forth is spoken from without.

The kingdom of heaven is within, and the keys which unlock this kingdom to the consciousness of man are the good words or words of God which we speak. We must speak the words that are true of Being, then will the true become manifest, and the false will pass away.

Not only does it take faith to disregard the appearance and call forth the ideal, but it takes a continuance of faith to establish the ideal in consciousness and make it real in experience. The word we speak is but a seed. Like every seed it grows first beneath the soil, hidden from view. When the seed-word is spoken it takes root in the soil of the mind. It will surely bring forth after its kind, and we will "reap in due time, . . if we faint not."

Often we miss the fruit of faith because we have not continued in faith, or awaited the fulfillment of faith. No farmer would plant his grain and not await his harvest. Instead he would make preparation for his harvest. He would plant his seed believing that he would receive.

Even so a mother who has conceived a child trusts that interior growth which takes place and which is hid from her view, and prepares for the birth of the child, believing she has received.

So, when we speak the word of Truth which is the seed of the ideal we wish to see manifest, we must believe we have, and with no doubt in the mind, trust that first growth which always takes place within, hid from view. Fear, doubt and uncertainty prevent the perfect "holding in mind" of the thing desired, and until it is established, or made firm, in mind it cannot take form in the external.

**"What can one do, who is a victim of past mistakes,** to rid himself of his undesirable conditions?" "Just change the thought; try to realize the mistakes . . stop thinking failure and suggest optimism." "I wish you would tell me how to stop thinking a thing which is always in front of one?" "Easy. Just don't see; become blind to all without and realize only the beauties of the great within, which is Truth itself." "Easier said than done, I am afraid, for the way is dark to me, I tell you." "Ah, my friend, the way can never be dark to him whose inner consciousness is lit by spiritual illumination."

"But how can I gain this great height which seems so far away? How am I, who has never realized the truth of a spiritual illumination, to enter that state of mind in which I see, feel and know this that you are saying is a 'Truth,' a 'Divine Truth'?" "Become as a little child, lay aside your previous beliefs; all prejudice; all the authorities of great men and the opinion of friends and stand forth alone, leaning not upon the broken staff of another for support. No longer pin your blind faith to the opinion of others, but let wisdom mount the throne of reason and become a willing pupil to the inner consciousness, and as the wheel of evolution slowly evolves you will become conscious of the omnipresent mind, the I AM part of you, which will lead you on and on until all is clear to your hitherto befogged vision."

**C. W. Kyle's - Concentration, the Key to Constructive Thought**

**(A lesser known classic in metaphysical literature)**

**3 Chapters (only)**

**1. The Silence, The Source of Power,**

**2. The Eternal Surprise**

**&**

**3. The Law of Success and Failure**

## C. W. Kyle

## 1. The Silence, The Source of Power

To be able to go into the Silence at will should be the aim of the student. Before one is enabled to do this, however, the control of the mind must be perfected. It requires that thinking shall have become a habit; a habit so fixed that one may, on the moment, become so concentrated that their every energy and attention may be given unreservedly to the subject in mind. This control is freedom. A freedom of action that shuts out sight and sound of the exterior world and holds the senses, by the power of concentration, with a firm grip, to the subject under consideration. For the free use of such power we should ever strive until attained.

> Freedom! oh, what would this world be,
> If Freedom sat upon the Heights!
> To rule one's self is to be free,
> How few yet taste of her delights!

It is one thing to control the mind thus, and it is another and quite as important an achievement, to be able to hold the mind in a state of absolute quietness; to remain alert and not think; to be so profoundly stilled that no wayward thought of the lower mind may enter.

This is no metaphysical form of ideation, but, on the other hand, it is the highest, the most practical and desirable state the human consciousness may reach, where thoughts wholly apart and distinct from subjects one may have previously been considering, flash into the mind with a strength and clearness that sets them in a class by themselves. In this manner alone may the universal intelligence be contacted, and to lead men to this ultimate source of wisdom and power should our most ear nest efforts be put forth.

One of the master thinkers of the age just past, whose mental impress stamps itself indelibly upon the highest form of the civilization of the present, in speaking of this state of consciousness said: Any person who has made observations on the state and progress of the human mind, by observing his own, cannot but have observed that there are two distinct classes of what are called Thoughts; those that we produce in ourselves by reflection and the act of thinking, and those that bolt into the mind of their own accord. I have always made it a rule to treat those voluntary visitors with civility, taking care to examine, as well as I was able, if they were worth entertaining; and it is from them I have acquired almost all the knowledge that I have."

To raise our consciousness to a plane where by reason of that which it has come to be, it attracts "voluntary visitors" from the higher planes of intelligence, is to make the most of our abilities, demonstrating as it does, the truth of the saying, "To him that hath more shall be given," not as a favor, but because he has complied with the law governing the growth of consciousness.

Do you wish wisdom? Do you wish for health, for wealth, for happiness, for power, for peace, for love? Here is the only avenue open to you whereby you may obtain the actual realization of your desires. It is the one thing in all the whole world worth striving for, for in grasping this, in making sure of your connection with the Source of All, you are placed in possession of "Aladdin's Lamp" and the "Philosopher's Stone." In other words, you have arrived.

There is nothing mysterious about this method of bringing the mind to function consciously within all of these separate states of consciousness . . separate only in the sense of an ever increasing realization of power. It is the plain, normal advancement of the intellect, absolutely sane, and in the most exacting sense scientific. You may come to know it for yourself; to realize in the most practical way the truth of it, and to receive and enjoy for yourself all of the inestimable powers and benefits this mastership of mind confers. It is all you can ever wish for or expect in the human consciousness. It is not difficult of attainment, if you determine to possess yourself of it. It requires the exercise of all your common sense in a concentrated degree, for it includes thinking, expressing and living your highest conceptions of truth.

Nothing wants you unless you first want it. You attract what you are. If you want anything you must, in essence, become that thing, when the supreme law of attraction, of growth, will be put in operation against which there is no power that can keep you from the thing you may desire. You are a supreme magnet in the great field of cosmic energy, charged with the power to draw your own to yourself.

The result of the highest revelation, using that word in the plain sense and meaning that whenever any fact that was unknown to us is made known, that it is revealed, shows that there is but one substance; that mind is universal, and, consequently in everything; that thought is the creator, and that all that is, is the product of thought.

All things spring from one source, and that source being infinite, it follows that nothing ever was or ever can be separated from it; space when used in this connection being an illusion. Everything, percept, concept, thought, form and act is included in the infinite. Infinity can have nothing opposed to it. "We only oppose ourselves from a lack of the knowledge of Unity.

The expression of Jesus, "I and my Father are one," clearly sets out his understanding of the truth of Unity. Harmony, peace and perfection are meaningless words unless founded upon the presupposition of Unity, and a lack of the understanding of this law and its application, has been the cause of all the trouble in the world. A comprehension of this law constitutes the supreme lesson for man to learn.

The physical man is the outer form of an inner concept and image, and so intimately connected are his bodies, of which he has seven, that there may be said to be no clear line of division between them; each one of them being "put on" and "put off" as the spirit has use for them. Each of these bodies is provided with receiving and distributing centers through which the life force flows, and when working in harmony the man is in full possession of all the forces that go to make of life a round of happiness, of health, of success and love.

The physical body is a perfect battery, composed of brain centers, and a perfect system of nerves which receive and transmit, according as they are attuned, all of the higher vibrations of which they are capable, hence, the importance of the injunction, "Get in tune with yourself," for all the life there is; all the intelligence there is, and all the power there is, and all the love there is, is pouring in upon you all the time, and you are free to register so much of it as you are cap able of doing.

By an understanding of the law you may function in each of these bodies as you will. You, the Thinker, are the ruler of them all, and to come to know the powers of your mastership and exercise them wisely, is the one great object of life. Discord, disease, and all inharmony arises from the lack of the normal adjustment of the nerve centers of the physical body and from its inharmonious relations with the finer bodies within it.

Until physical science shall come to understand the co-relation and inter dependence of man's several bodies; their interpenetration and the separate uses of each of them, it will be at a loss to account for excrescent growths, malformations and many diseases, especially of nervous disorders, irregularities of the heart, and mental disorders of a temporary nature, including a multitude of mental afflictions running from morbidness to feeble mindedness and from imbecility to insanity.

If the subconscious mind, or "psychic self," as the inner body has been denominated, becomes abnormal, changing its relations to the physical body, from any cause, the most serious results may be expected to ensue.

Negative thinking and indulging the emotional nature to excess is the primary cause of all these disturbances. The present condition of the race at tests how very inadequate is the attempt to treat these disorders from the physical side of life only. The normal relations of these bodies must be brought about before harmonious results may be expected, and as disordered thoughts caused the inharmony, constructive thought must be aroused that order may be restored. This is best done, as is well known, by inducing natural rest and sleep during which undisturbed condition the life force re adjusts the disordered relations and normal action ensues.

During sleep the negative thoughts no longer disturb and the results of their former action are most easily overcome by giving Nature's restoring powers the opportunity to work their will unhindered; the patient sleeps, perspires, and the danger is past. What has occurred? The negative mind has been stilled, and the exterior forces have ceased to trouble, giving the inner forces of the man the opportunity to do the healing and restoring work. This is the object of all methods of drugless healing.

The power by which you govern all of this marvelous machinery through which life is expressed is THOUGHT. "As a man thinketh in his heart so is he." If you desire health, THINK HEALTH; if you desire wealth THINK WEALTH, and if you desire LOVE, THINK LOVE, always THINK LOVE for it fulfills every requirement of the law; it meets every possible demand that may be made upon you, and it clears the way of all obstructions.

Concentration is the method by which you will win the desire of your heart; it matters not what your trouble may be, concentrated thought will bring you sure and perfect relief. By the positive exercise of thought are you made just What you are and by its exercise you may become whatsoever you will to be.

The object and purpose of going into the Silence is that we may contact the higher vibrations . . to come in touch with the Source of Universal Energy and Power. Herein lies the secret of all becoming, for here we are enabled to catch all that we may be enabled to express of the Divinity of being. Happy is he who has found this never failing oasis in the otherwise comparatively lifeless desert of human experience.

When you contact this supreme state you will know it; you will never have a doubt about that experience, for no flash of lightning, however vivid, could have impressed you so much as will this first experience. When you once have experienced the effect of contacting this powerful voltage, you will no longer be enslaved by the bonds of the psychic mind. From the indolent state of the subjective . . the world of idle fancies and dreams, in which the many are content to dwell . . you will be carried into a practical, sane and sensible plane of life where the power which you have received will call into activity every energy of your whole nature, and your life of action and genuine worth to yourself and others will begin.

"We awake to the consciousness of it, we are aware of it (this indefinable plus) coming forth in our mind; but we feel that we did not make it, that it is discovered to us, that it is whether we will or no."

Thoughts are things of force and power,<br>
I feel and know this saying true,<br>
For but within the present hour,<br>
They swift have flown to me from you

## C. W. Kyle

## 2. The Eternal Surprise

There is a power latent in every man which, when aroused, changes him at once into another being. It thrills, awakens and transforms him into a new man, making of him a veritable dynamo of tremendous energy. His conscious identity with this newly awakened power is amazing, and the use he makes of it astonishes all who have previously known him.

From a man of inaction he becomes a leader. He seeks advice from no one, but realizing his awakened powers he relies upon himself, and goes forward sustained with a confidence and enthusiasm, nothing doubting, to the accomplishment of his own desires.

He has become an awakened soul, knowing and fearlessly exercising his newly realized powers of dominion. He knows just what he wants; he is determined to get it and he goes out and gets it. He has come to know himself.

The supreme lesson of life is that of self-realization.

You are living in a world of magic. You have more power within you than that ever recorded of any genii of whom you have ever read or dreamed. Wake up ! Learn who you are before you condemn yourself to a further life of inaction and inefficiency.

To come to recognize yourself is the best elixir of life you will ever know. It will take a psychological operation to rid you of your self-imposed limitations. Well, here it is. Words have a magic power. The greatest event in all the record that infinite intelligence has made, was manifest by the power of the Word. "In the beginning was the Word and the Word was with God and the Word was God." What is the meaning of that? It means that God pictured in Mind all that is, and then spoke it into actuality, creating man in His own image, an individualized center of His every attribute . . consciousness, creative power and love.

Did you never pause to think that man is the only instrument God has fashioned through which His word may be most fitly spoken? The man who has not come to realize this truth is apt to find that most of the paths of life lead down to the bottom of the hill, where those who have taken them lie bound by their own thoughts of limitation, which are more powerful to imprison than though made of steel. If you are there, awake and burst your bonds ! Stand forth free and rejoice in your strength, for you are the ruling Prince in the House of the King of Kings.

To come to recognize yourself is to experience the greatest event you will ever know. Though you may be presented at court and dine with the king, that event will be as nothing of importance to you beside it; though the king should bestow all honors upon you within his power, they will prove in consequential, compared to the wonderful honors you will find awaiting you, when you come to know yourself.

You are a king and a creator in your own right. You have made yourself just what you are, and you have the power to change yourself into a being greater and more powerful than it is possible for you to conceive. You are possessed of unlimited powers, and if limited you now are, you, yourself, have raised the walls of limitation, and you have power to remove them or you may let them stand. You are ruler of your own kingdom.

When you come to know yourself as you are, the very splendid powers which are yours will awaken in you such respect for them that you will feel called upon to live at your very best, at all times, in order to be worthy of the high dignity of your position in life. This knowledge will put new blood in your veins and a song of joy in your heart. Your whole being will be filled and thrilled with a sense of being so much greater than that you have ever felt before, that no thought of fear or failure will ever again find lodgment in your mind.

Love and faith and courage will shine out in your every word and act, and dignity will mantle you as one to the purple born; the light of kindly determination will fill your eyes and you will be fired with an enthusiasm that will render you invincible, where before you have been faltering and filled with indecision.

I Wish above all else to introduce you to yourself . . the real man that you are, and have you see yourself as you were made in the image of God, endowed with His every attribute, and in actual possession of all the tools wherewith to make yourself greater than any conception of greatness that has ever entered into the heart of man.

Don't refuse the offer of this acquaintanceship, for the one great lack of man upon this planet, the one thing in which he stands in direst need, is nothing more or less than a more intimate and thorough acquaintanceship with himself.

If I may, even in a small way, be instrumental in furthering your acquaintanceship with yourself, I feel assured that I shall ever stand high on the list of your cherished friends.

I am aware that it may appear presumptuous on my part to assume the role of one intimate enough with your life to make bold to introduce you to any person, to say nothing of the implied knowledge on my part and the lack of it on yours, to undertake to introduce you to yourself. It may be, however, that the awakened curiosity in your minds as to how I have acquired sufficient knowledge of you to assume to introduce you to yourself, will cause you to refrain from taking offense.

Again, it is generally assumed that one who introduces one person to another stands as sponsor for the one introduced, a responsibility, I have no doubt that each one of you have, at one time or another, found to be more or less embarrassing. In this case, I hasten to assure you, that I cheerfully assume full responsibility, for the personage I would introduce to you is worthy of the highest honors you may bestow, and one whom you will feel highly honored to know. If you will cultivate his acquaintanceship, and be guided by his advice, whatsoever of good you may desire will come to you.

Concentration will enable you to further this acquaintanceship as nothing else can. The young man who had fall en to the level of the swine, "came to himself," and felt no need of asking the advice of any one, and if you are, living a life short of the realization of your best desires you should come to yourself, and know that "the kingdom of God is within you," and that if you will only concentrate upon it earnestly enough, and long enough, that you shall here and now come into possession of and enjoy every good your heart may desire.

Health, wealth, honor, power, station, peace and love are awaiting the exercise of the powers that you possess, in order to be and abide with you, just so long as you may will them to remain.

When man comes to know that he is the being of power, intelligence and love that he truly is; that he is master of his own thoughts, and that he has access to the Source of Infinite Life, his thoughts take on a splendor and beauty which finds their expression in living every moment of his life at its best. He finds that all intelligent choice and necessity of action, to be one and the same; that the right way of thinking is the only way open to the man of the enlightened mind; that all growth is, in its final expression, upwards, and that consciousness is ever passing from a lower to a higher plane and in so doing that a sane, sensible and normal life is assured by maintaining a state of equilibrium between his inner sense and his environment.

We are free to select the thoughts with which we feed our minds, more free than we are in selecting the foods with which we feed our bodies. This is well, for the character of our thoughts is far more important to our health and happiness than the nature of the foods we eat.

Clean thoughts not only make clean minds but they also make clean, healthy bodies. A body ruled by a strong, clean mind is best fortified against all of the current ills of life.

Your thoughts build into your body the very sub stance of which it is composed. Thoughts of envy, malice, hatred and all thoughts that lead to despondency, devitalize the blood and affect the body ruinously. Anger is a positive poison to the blood, while thoughts of kindness, cheerfulness and good-will are powerful tonics, stimulating digestion, and contribute, in the most wonderful way, to the harmonious working of all the vital organs of our bodies.

When man comes to realize the power of mastership which he wields over his body he will become more cautious in his thinking than in his handling of sharpened tools. He will send out only thoughts of strength, of health, of harmony and love. "When he learns to do this he will find that his bodily intelligence will respond promptly and eagerly, every cell in his whole system taking in the full force and character of his thought and, if he has thought wisely and constructively, he will find his body to be a radiant expression of all that he has commanded it to be.

Extreme as these statements may at first glance appear, they will be found upon examination to be the most practical and useful truths of life.

Thought wedded to purpose is the only way by which our plans may be carried out. It is impossible for us to set too high a standard for our thoughts. Man finds himself a weak, vacillating creature, without purpose because he has been taught that he is a weak, negative creature. It is high time that his attention be called to the possibilities of his being, when his la tent powers are aroused and placed in action.

Wherein lie the powers of dominion said to have been given man, unless by the power of the awakened spirit within him, he may make all conditions to serve him? We know that success comes only to the man who has a definite object, who thinks strongly and who strives earnestly and fearlessly in the battle of life. The man who marks a straight line from his desire to its realization and who permits no allurements to draw him aside, is the man who wins. No man who has not done so, may, or should succeed.

To permit a doubt to enter the mind as to the essential unity of the human soul with the source of all power, all intelligence and all love, is to render every effort ineffectual; to cloud the mind and to paralyze the arm and, in a word, to invite inevitable disaster and defeat.

Why, then, should the intelligent investigator stop short of accepting and announcing the inevitable conclusion to which he is driven? Doubt, fear and prejudice and all products of negative thought, when allowed to enter the mind, drive out constructive thinking by devitalizing the mind of its power and energy. A knowledge of what we can do must precede the effort to do.

## C. W. Kyle

## 3. The Law of Success and Failure

Concentration is success. The concentrated man radiates success, breathes it, attracts it by the action of a law as certain in its operation as the law which causes the water to run down hill. The will of a thoroughly concentrated man is the most powerful force that life has expressed upon this planet. He does that which he wills to do, and in the doing of the act he illustrates one of the fundamental laws of life.

The very act of man's desiring anything, sets in operation the law by which he is bound to realize his desire. Desiring anything attests that that thing is somewhere awaiting the call of your desire, that it may come in answer to your call, for it is a truth demonstrated by all the expressions of nature that the object of your desire on its part most strongly desires you The very fact of being throughout all the kingdoms of nature, illustrates the operation of this law. Minerals of a kind attract each other; plants of a kind grow side by side; animals of a kind have the same habitat, going in pairs or droves, and, in a more extended sense than the surface meaning of the words convey, "Birds of a feather flock together."

The operation of this law lies at the base of everything. The atom or electron, however small, could not be without cohesion. It is held together, and around it is built, by the operation of this same law, every manifestation that appears in all Nature. This same law that rules the atom, rules in the kingdom of mind where every desire is found to attract its own, first building a perfect form in mind and then realizing it in the outer physical world. This is creation as it has ever been, as it now is, and, as it will continue to be. You may ignore the law and go on blundering through life, at best, realizing only a small measure of success, when an understanding of the law and an intelligent cooperation with it would have given you the full measure of your de sires.

The inevitables of nature await our understanding of and cooperation with them, and we will find, sooner or later, that the freedom which we so much de sire awaits our understanding of and obedience to the laws inherent within our own being. To this end, the law scourges and prods and drives us ever on and on, having in view the development of the perfect man.

It is this same law, demonstrating that man attracts what he is, that enables the artist to catch" glimpses of the absolute . . the overtones of our normal state of consciousness, and express them in architecture, sculpture, painting, poetry, the drama or music, thus giving to his work a universal and imperishable quality which stamps it as true art. He attracts all because there is in all that which is within himself, he having contacted and expressed the universal law.

The creation and realization of one's ideals are alterating divisions on the path of unfoldment, evidencing the effort to clothe one's inner conceptions with an outward garment; fashioning the next step upon which to mount.

Beethoven, in the creation of his deathless symphonies, experienced the power of thought to control and heal the body as evidenced by his writing these words: "I do not fear for my works. No evil can befall them; and whosoever shall understand them, he shall be freed from all the miseries that burden mankind." The wonderful power of music as a healing agent, now universally recognized, is accounted for by its tendency to make us concentrate. Everyone has, doubtless, realized the truth expressed by Balzac where he says : "Music alone of all the arts, has power to make us live within ourselves." This quality of music is its greatest worth, as it teaches us that the dominant object of life is the recognition of the true self . . the only way by which we may unfold . . as all growth is from within.

The man who thinks, knows that his body is but the instrument of his thought, and that he can cleanse it of disease by thought as certainly as he cleans the pen with which he writes.

Some years since I became acquainted with a man who looked upon the world with an eye less of distrust than that of indifference. He had traveled over the world, being driven by the spirit of unrest until he had become tired of it all. He had turned with feelings of equal lack of interest from the Great Pyramids of Egypt and the art galleries of Europe; he had thrown himself into the wildest forms of excitement known to men, working with pick and pan in the gold fields of Australia and Alaska, only to find that the raging fever, the grip of the mad lust for gold, which drove other men frantic, passed him by without arousing in him but a fleeting interest. It seemed that he had arrived at a state of mind where he could look upon any phase of life's activities and say, "Oh, what's the use."

He was strong, healthy and dependent upon his daily labor for his living.

One evening he dropped in at a meeting where I was talking to the members of the "Happy Thought Club." 1 dwelt upon the importance of concentration as a means of furnishing an un failing interest in life, when everything else had lost power to attract emphasizing the idea that to know yourself was to solve the problem of what to do with yourself. He talked with me on several occasions after that and then disappeared.

While passing through the down town district of San Francisco, a few months since, a gentleman approached me, exclaiming, "Where on earth have you been keeping yourself? I have inquired of many of your former acquaintances, but could get no trace of you. Come to my office," he insisted, "I've something to say to you there." In a few moments we had entered into a well equipped business office where every appearance spelled "SUCCESS"; you could catch that at a glance. Passing into his private office, he turned with a smile, saying, "I wanted to show you this," letting his eyes rove over the office, "and to say that I am doing a very satisfactory business. I've won; any man on the street will tell you that, and I have done it where others have failed. I owe it all to you. It was your way of pointing out to me the fact that every man must find himself, before life could open up to him anything of more than passing interest. I simply found myself and went to work doing that which I found I could most easily do."

He was most grateful. He went on to say that he was happily married and had become the proud father of two lovely children; that he owned a comfortable home within an hour's ride from the city. "I have found it comparatively easy to carry out your ideas in the constructive sense, but I cannot at times, help thinking how very foolish I was to waste so many years of my life just for the want of knowing what to do with myself."

After receiving a pressing invitation to visit him at his home, I left him, and as I walked down the street the familiar saying of the ages kept running through my mind: "And some seed fell upon good ground."

I have never known a more thorough change to have come to any man than to this one. Prom an aimless state of absolute indifference he has become a thorough and efficient business man, always cheerful and happy with as great an interest in life as any one whom I know. He found it worthwhile to become acquainted with himself.

The efficiency which is to be derived from a knowledge of the laws of concentration is definitely attested by a very successful insurance man who said that for years he was troubled with a hesitancy at times that almost unfitted him for business. He told me how he had become interested in the methods which were being given to fortify one's courage. "I could not at first believe," said he, "that in so simple a matter as you suggest lay anything that could materially assist me in my work. But when I began to put it to the test I was surprised at the results. Now, I never approach any one on business without first fortifying myself with the strength which your methods induce. It gives a man faith and confidence in himself and in the business he is doing."

It is the creative power which thought alone can demonstrate, that gives faith and courage. To BELIEVE IN ONE'S SELF and in one's work is the very foundation of

SUCCESS. I know of no more striking example of supreme courage than that shown by Lincoln Beachey, the aviator, who so concentrated upon his work as to fill every cell of his body with courage, enabling him to do that which no other man in America had ever dared to attempt. To rise to the height of a mile above the earth, and there turn the airplane upside down in a series of loops, for the first time in the history of one's country, requires a mental control and a FAITH IN ONE'S OWN POWERS that must challenge the admiration of mankind.

Had we such faith in the powers of the mind to control the body, disease would speedily disappear from the earth. Thought is the CAUSE, not the RESULT.

> I AM, this truth I feel and know;
> All that I AM or yet may be,
> Through my own consciousness must
> flow,
> Be it of high or low degree.
> I AM, and hold within my power
> The choice to winnow well the grain
> Of life's rich harvest, and each hour,
> Drive from my life disease and pain.
> I AM, and know that "this" or "that"
> Is not myself nor ere can be;
> The "I" that "AM" has ever sat
> From time and change forever free.
> I AM, and with the boundless real . .
> Hope, faith and love, shall grow supreme;
> All consciousness shall yet reveal
> Glories more vast than I can dream.
> I AM, and with all love and truth,
> Shall find from care a sure release,
> When wisdom's age and strength of youth,
> Be crowned with everlasting peace.

# 12 Meditations

# from

# U. S. Andersen's

# Three Magic Words

# Meditation 1

I know that I AM pure spirit, that I always have been, and that I always will be. There is inside me a place of confidence and quietness and security where all things are known and understood. This is the Universal Mind, God, of which I AM a part and which responds to me as I ask of it. This Universal Mind knows the answer to all of my problems, and even now the answers are speeding their way to me. I needn't struggle for them; I needn't worry or strive for them. When the time comes, the answers will be there. I give my problems to the great mind of God; I let go of them, confident that the correct answers will return to me when they are needed. Through the great law of attraction, everything in life that I need for my work and fulfillment will come to me. It is not necessary that I strain about this – only believe. For in the strength of my belief, my faith will make it so. I see the hand of divine intelligence all about me, in the flower, the tree, the brook and the meadow. I know that the intelligence that created all these things is in me and around me and that I can call upon it for my slightest need. I know that my body is a manifestation of pure spirit and that spirit is perfect; therefore my body is perfect also. I enjoy life, for each day brings a constant demonstration of the power and wonder of the universe and myself. I AM confident. I AM serene. I AM sure. No matter what obstacle or undesirable circumstance crosses my path, I refuse to accept it, for it is nothing but illusion. There can be no obstacle or undesirable circumstance to the mind of God, which is in me, and around me, and serves me now.

# Meditation 2

I know that I AM one with the Universal Mind. I know this mind is perfect and I may rely upon it for complete guidance in all of my daily affairs. This Universal Mind, this great Subconscious Mind, this mind of God knows no evil or limitation or lack. It simply creates in my experience that which I believe and accept. Therefore I deny all evil and all error. When my eyes and my senses are deluded with the apparent circumstance of evil, I turn away, lifting my thoughts to the perfection and abundance and love of all the universe. I know that God does not create evil; and I know that by using the power of God I AM able to deny evil, which is only illusion, simply error, and will not stand before truth. For the great reality is good, which is always attempting to manifest itself. I know that error or evil is the result of my own thought, is the result of error on my part, is the result of isolating myself from the power of the Universal Mind. I know that the Universal Mind is constantly creating in my experience that which I think, and if evil is manifested, it has come from my own thought; and my own thought may as quickly deny it. I do not will anything to happen, for I AM not bigger than God. I simply understand that the law of creation is bigger than I AM and that I cannot help my thoughts and beliefs from becoming real in my experience. Therefore I hold my thoughts steadfastly on the good. I do not do this with effort, as if I were commanding something to act. I simply relax in contemplation of the good, secure in the knowledge that everything rests with a power much greater than I AM. I trust this power. I have complete faith and confidence in this power. I rely upon this power for guidance in all my daily affairs. I refuse to accept evil, and evil is gone. I accept good, and the supply and love of the universe are mine.

# Meditation 3

I know and recognize my oneness with all things. I know that all form and all circumstance are the creation of an infinite intelligence that is in and around me. I know that all things are the result of conception and desire, that my world is ordered according to my own thoughts and convictions. Therefore I concentrate on harmony. I see nothing but order and constructiveness all about me. I do not accept thoughts of destructiveness and disharmony. In my friends, my loved ones, my fellow workers, I see nothing but cooperation and assistance. I know that we all seek: the same answers and the same goals. I know that each person must follow a different path toward his vision, and I understand the searching and the copings of everyone I know and see. I have sympathy and tolerance for all things and all people. I know that in as much as I help others I help myself. In my brother's eye there is my own soul. In my friend's smile there is my own humor. In my neighbor's sorrow there is my own loss. I have compassion and understanding for all things, for this life in which I have my being strives for understanding of itself. I deny error; it is simply progress toward truth. I know that it is impossible to fail when faith is present. I do not order things to be made in my time or in my place, but trust the Universal Mind in its own great knowledge of the time and the place and the need and the way. Each moment of each day brings my life closer to realization. The objects of my work are being accomplished this very minute. Success and harmony, peace and confidence are mine.

# Meditation 4

I know that all of life exists within me. Here in my heart and mind, in the recesses of my being, there is utter calm, a place of unruffled and placid waters, where the truth is apparent and the clamor of the world does not exist. I see about me the thoughts of all mankind, for these thoughts have become things. Whatever is good among these thought-things I accept; whatever is evil I ignore; for my concern is only with truth and understanding, which is forever the lovely and the good and the expanding. My mind moves easily to the further most reaches of space, in all directions, and just as easily moves back to me once again. I AM the center of the universe. God, the Universal Subconscious Mind, has made himself manifest through me. I know that my purpose in life is to reach ever upward and outward, to expand in knowledge and love and unity. I place my future in divine hands. I turn over each problem of my life to that great all-knowing mind to which all things are possible. I do not tell God how to bring these things about. I have complete confidence that every circumstance that comes my way is part of a perfect plan to convert the image of my faith into physical reality. Even now the universe seeks to answer my every need. As I believe in my heart, so shall it be done unto me; this is the law of life and of living. There is greatness in my friend and in my enemy, for we are all brothers seeking the same high mountain along many paths. God, who made all creatures, made no poor creature, for He made only of himself. I AM prosperous for God owns everything. I AM vigorous for God is all vigor. I need only open my mind and my heart, keep my thoughts in the path of truth, and I AM filled to overflowing with the power and abundance and love of the universe.

# Meditation 5

I listen to the voice of the universe as it speaks within me. It is the voice of truth and it guides me unerringly along the paths of my life. Somewhere deep within me, in the perfect bud of my soul, there stands an immobile universe where all things and all law lie revealed. I reach within to this place of peace and quietness. I listen to the voice of my heart. I close my eyes and sense a living, breathing universe dwelling within me, and I dwelling in it. I AM one with all people and all life and all things. I move in accordance with divine law. All the limitless power of creation is mine to draw upon, for it is in me and one with me and I AM a part of it. The answer comes with the question; the path is lighted with the first step; the way is cleared with the looking; the goal is in sight with the desire. I know that I AM fulfilling the fondest wish of God, for I place myself in His hands, taking each step of my life boldly and strongly, for it is God who prompts me, and God moves with sureness. I see tomorrow for I know today, and this day is father of tomorrow. The things of my life are the children of my thoughts, and my thoughts of today are even now bearing the children of tomorrow. All that is good I desire; all that is evil I refuse to accept. By attaining, I do not deprive. All that is and ever will be is available to every man; he need only ask and it shall be given. I bind myself to the power for good that surges heavenward all around me. The limits and inhibitions of my past are gone. Each day is a new birth of my soul. Each day is another step on my journey to a oneness with God. I do not seek, I know. I do not strive, I AM guided.

# Meditation 6

Here in solitude, in this time of peace, of meditation, I withdraw deep into the silent recesses of my being to a place of utter calm. Slowly the world retreats from around me, until finally I AM alone. Walled away from all clamor and strife there is nothing but me. I AM not body; I AM not thought; I AM not experience; I AM not the past nor the present nor the future. I simply AM. Across my consciousness comes a constant procession of thoughts and I observe them. I do not make up these thoughts. I know they come from the Universal Subconscious Mind, and I watch as they are presented to me. I slow the train of thoughts. I examine each of them, then let go, neither accepting nor rejecting. On and on the thoughts come, and I ask myself, "Who is it that observes this?" And I hear the answer, "Thou that art, always have been, and always will be . . thou observes!," and I understand. Divorced from body, thought, and experience, I still exist as I always must. Here then is my true self, a thing independent of all but spirit, a contemplative "I," which only observes and chooses from the thoughts that cross consciousness. Whatever I choose is mine. Whatever I reject shall never touch me. I need only observe and accept, and all things will be added unto me by a power which leaps to acknowledge my faith and my decision. I sense such warmth and security as might overflow the world. I sense a fusion of my being with the great Universal Subconscious Mind, the mind of God. I sense the presence of the Father who knows no wrath, who does all things at his child's bidding. I sense my union with this Father by immutable and irrevocable bonds. I AM one with all truth, all beauty, all justice, all love.

# Meditation 7

I do not confuse what I seem to be with what I really AM. I AM never what I seem to be, and always what I really AM . . host to the indwelling God. I quiet the movements of my body, slow my breathing, and glide deep into the recesses of my being, to the very center of my consciousness. Here in this place of infinite calm I become one with the immortal Self of the world, and I observe. My thoughts cross my consciousness in a never-ending stream. I do not create these thoughts. They come from the infinite reaches of the Universal Subconscious Mind and are directed to my consciousness, for I have attracted them. I may choose any thoughts I desire. I have but to decide, and the ideas and images I have chosen are directed to me. As I accept them so will they manifest in my world. I alone decide what I will think; thus I decide my entire life. I bar the door of my mind to negative thoughts or thoughts of evil. The door is always open to admit the positive, the good, the beautiful and the aspiring. I have complete confidence in the wisdom and the power of the Universal Subconscious Mind. I do not predict the manner in which each of my thoughts will manifest; I have complete faith that God moves in the most perfect manner. There is no such thing as lack unless it is accepted; the universe has infinite supply. Vigor and health, abundance and success are mine, for I choose only such thoughts. Love abounds in a universe where I AM one with the immortal Self, the Universal Subconscious Mind, God. My every decision is answered from a perfect and inexhaustible source of power.

# Meditation 8

The truth about life is the infinite love of God for all things. Each man is my brother, bound to me by immortal and everlasting ties. I love all people; they dwell in my Father and my Father in them. I surrender my heart to humanity, and humanity serves me with love. I surrender my heart to God, and the love of God becomes complete in me. I AM one with all the power and vigor and knowledge of the universe. I let go of fear and confusion; They are illusions and cannot live with truth, which is love, which is complete and fulfilled in me now. The great reality of Universal Subconscious Mind is forever present at the center of my being. I draw from it perfect intelligence, perfect health, perfect peace, perfect happiness, perfect love. I surrender all the built up inhibitions that have been impressed upon me by the illusions of the world. I refuse to accept anything but truth, which is always the good and the positive. I move in accord with Divine Intelligence. I accept the will and the love of God, which I express in laughter and joy and pleasure and service. Only the good, the great, the significant, and the constructive do I add unto myself. Nothing else is allowed into the creative depths of my being. The surging desire of each man is to know the fulfillment of love. The way to this fulfillment is through contact with the center of consciousness, through communion with the silent dweller within. I surrender my doubts and confusions and fears. Universal love is complete in me. I AM united with God, move with God. I AM serene and sure, joyful and achieving, confident of ultimate splendor.

# Meditation 9

The infinite creative power of the Universal Subconscious Mind lies within me. I attune myself; remove all barriers from my thought, become receptive to the purposes of God. I know that my life is great and good when I perform service with love. The right ideas are delivered to me, I accept them and Subconscious Mind provides me with the means of bringing them into my world. I know that all things spring from Universal Mind, which is infinitely abundant. Lack and limitation are errors in thinking and I banish them from my consciousness. There can be no lack. I need only to let the Universal Mind express itself through me and my world is filled with creativeness, achievement and prosperity. My goal will be delivered to me for they are the goal of God who never fails. Whatever my task I perform it with love, for I know that when I serve another I serve the purposes of a greater design. All about me I see the law of mutual exchange therefore I give as I would receive. I know that abundance and prosperity are mental conditions. I create them on the plane of mind with complete trust and confidence that they will manifest in my life. I refuse to accept undesirable circumstance as having final reality. First cause is mental and is never found in the world about me. A mighty truth is at the center of my consciousness, w here no work is difficult, where peace always reigns, where all things are possible. I know that life is a journey that must be traveled step by step and I AM patient, enjoying the wonder of the way with unshakable faith in my destination. I submit my will, knowing that success will come when I fulfill my indwelling self.

# Meditation 10

My body is a manifestation of my knowledge of myself and my true self is spirit, is consciousness only and is invisible. Other people see me not. They see but my body. It is only I who know myself and this knowledge returns to me in my health and in the things of my life. Therefore I affirm that my spirit is perfect, that I AM one with the great self of the universe. The energy of this great self permeates my being, cleanses me of all impurities of the flesh, restores every function of body to perfect harmony. There is perfect elimination, perfect assimilation. My entire being is spiritual and my body is quickened into new life with the perception of this great truth. I surrender myself to the wisdom and guidance of the Universal Subconscious Mind. I become one with the purpose of God and this mighty purpose animates my body, projects into every aspect of my life. There is no obstruction, no barrier, no limitation in my mind. I see only peace, power, vigor and plenty. I open my heart to love and love flows through every atom and pore of my body, energizing, molding and coordinating. My healing my mind of limitation and lack and negative thinking, I automatically heal my body. At the center of my being, I perceive limitless, ageless and deathless spirit, perfect in beauty, perfect in function. This spirit becomes manifest in my body and in my affairs. When I am faced with apparent confusion, I surrender it, give over each of my problems and worries to that which has the perfect solution and in which there is absolute clarity. I take my thoughts from the limitless reaches of Universal Subconscious Mind, never from the world around me. I do not think responsively, I think originally; I do not react, I act. I AM never a victim of circumstances, for each thing of my life proceeds from out of my thoughts, which move always in accord with God.

# Meditation 11

I know I AM pure spirit, deathless, changeless, birthless and eternal. I AM not body; I AM not conscious mind; I AM not ego. I AM sense of Self only, conscious, awareness, unadulterated being. The presence that animates all life is within me, is altogether the real me. I AM using my body for a purpose, as an expression of an idea and when the idea is fully expressed, through my work and my mission, I shall return again to unity with Universal Self, leaving body and ego behind. I do not confuse my body and ego with what I truly am. My body is simply and instrument for my expression and my ego is simply memory of physical experience. Returning to infinity and unity, I shall need neither body nor ego. I AM free of the domination of the ego. It is not my true self, it is simply an illusion necessary to finiteness and the perception of space and time. I turn away from the ego, withdraw into the depths of my being to the immortal consciousness that lies within. Here in this magic center, my word is law. I need only speak it with faith and conviction and it will manifest in my life. I AM calm and serene, sure and unfaltering, for my roots are in eternity. All the things of life shall change and pass away, but I shall never pass away, for wherever life is I shall be, one with Universal Subconscious Mind. I need not strive nor strand for attain immortality, nor fear punishment, nor aspire for reward. The kingdom of heaven awaits all, the wise, the foolish, the sinner and the saint, for we are all one in reality, clothed in different forms in this moment of incarnation. I do not fear death, for by it I attain the consciousness of higher Self. Neither do I invite death, for it must wait until my work is done. I forsake the ego, perceive self in Self, see the majesty, the grandeur, the immortality of the power that dwells within.

# Meditation 12

I turn away from the world about me to the world of consciousness that lies within. I shut out all memories of the past and create no images of the future. I concentrate on my being, on my awareness. I slide deep into the very recesses of my soul to a place of utter repose. Here I perceive fact in the making and I AM conscious of the one being from which all beings spring. I know that this is immortal Self, this is GOD, this is me. I AM, I always was, I always will be. All men, all things, all space and time and life are here in the depths of my soul. Smaller than small, greater than great meet and unite in me. That which I thought I was, ego, I never was at all, for it was a changing thing, mirroring the seasons and the tides, a thing to be born and grow and die. I AM not a thing of time and circumstance. I AM spirit, pure and eternal, birthless, deathless and changeless. I AM patient, for I AM all time: I AM wise, for I contain the knowledge of all things. I know not pain, for I see there is no beginning and no end and he who suffers pain must see beginning and end. I AM rich for there is no limit to the abundance I may create from my very Self. I AM successful, for I need only think to achieve. I AM loved and am beloved, all things are my Self and I AM all things. I unite, I fuse, I become one with Universal Subconscious Mind. The mask of vanity and ego I shall never wear again. I perceive the magnificent dweller at the center of my consciousness and I know him to be my very Self. Time and space, shadow and substance, what matter these? I AM GOD.

# Affirmations for Mastery

**Say often, as you go about your day**

**The more these are repeated, the more they become integrated into your life & the more they affect your life, in a positive manner.**

"You cannot command that which is not. As there is no other, you must command yourself to be that which you would have appear.

Let me clarify what I mean by effective command. You do not repeat like a parrot the statement, "I AM That I AM"; such vain repetition would be both stupid and fruitless.

It is not the words that make it effective; it is the consciousness of being the thing, which makes it effective.

When you say, "I AM", you are declaring yourself to be. The word that in the statement, "I AM That I AM", indicates that which you would be. The second "I AM" in the quotation is the cry of victory." - Neville

I AM God's highest ideal made manifest.

I AM a center of attraction.

"I AM the master of my fate, I AM the captain of my soul."

The I AM within you produces anything and everything.

There is only One Power of creation, and it is I AM, or consciousness, awareness, mind or imagery.

"Act as though I AM, and I will be."

"I AM constantly becoming healthier, stronger, younger and more successful."

I earnestly aspire to express the nobility of self control.

I AM determined to be the master of my moods.

I AM resolved to be constructive in my thoughts.

I AM conscious of an ever-growing poise.

I AM calm, serene and confident.

I AM daily growing in courage and power.

My power of will is steadily increasing.

I AM the master of my habits.

I gladly initiate new habits.

I AM open to new thoughts and new impressions.

I glory in the daily exercise of my constructive will.

I AM determined to be original, vital and versatile.

I will persistently look on the joyous side of life.

I invite and express strong, loving, helpful emotions.

The Divine Spirit inspires in me a serene faith.

I face the future with a courageous mind.

The power is within me to be truly efficient.

I think, clear, strong, creative thoughts.

I will persistently guide my emotions into life-giving channels.

I take joy in simple, natural, health giving exercise for mind and body.

I radiate sunshine to everyone I meet.

My memory is growing stronger year by year, and day by day.

I delight in exercise and nourishment for my memory by daily learning and vital facts.

My interest in life is growing stronger and stronger as the years go by.

My will to live is invincible.

I AM gaining clearer perception, stronger, keener, reasoning power.

I transmute my creative energies to regenerate life.

I radiate harmony, love and confidence to all.

I realize that every function of life is sacred and worthy of honor.

I breathe deeply and harmoniously of pure, abundant air.

I will make all my words express the one hundred per cent constructive life.

I AM prosperity.

I attract prosperity.

I radiate prosperity.

Prosperity is my birthright.

My success is assured.

My supply is plentiful.

I AM one with the Source.

I manifest riches.

Wealth is mine.

I think prosperity.

I talk prosperity.

I breathe prosperity.

My prosperity is inevitable.

Prosperity is for me here and now.

I AM Health

I AM Love

I AM Success

I AM Intelligence

I AM is Universal Mind.

I AM is Life.

I AM is Power.

I AM is Health.

I AM is Wealth.

I AM is Success.

I AM is Everything I AM or can be, for I AM the I AM!

I AM strong and well.

I AM a soul. I have a body.

All good things are within me.

I AM one with the Infinite.

I AM pure spirit, and spirit is perfect.

I AM filled with the fullness of life.

I AM filled with the spirit of health.

I AM perfectly free and always shall be.

I have perfect health in abundance.

I have life and power in abundance.

I AM well, I AM well, I AM well.

I AM strong, I AM strong, I AM strong.

I AM perfect in being, through and through.

I AM peace, I AM joy, I AM harmony.

Nothing but the good shall come to me.

I desire nothing but that which is good.

I AM pure and clean in thought and speech.

I shall seek only the right in every action.

My life is filled with the beautiful and the true.

I love everybody and desire everybody to love me.

I AM in harmony with every creature in existence.

Spirit is in perfect health, and I AM a spiritual being.

I AM always happy, for I AM living the life beautiful.

Peace, power and plenty are my constant companions.

My body is real and good, and all its functions are good.

The blessings of health, happiness and harmony are forever mine.

I AM the real man, and the real man is always well.

I know the truth and the truth has made me free.

I AM strong in the spirit, for invincible power is mine.
Infinite power is in me, for I AM one with the Supreme.

I can do what I will to do, for my life is my own.

I AM living the life of the spirit, the life of infinite good.

I AM born of Pure Spirit.

False ideas cannot be transmitted from one to another, and I AM free from race suggestion.

I AM Clean, Pure and Perfect, and my Word eliminates all else.

I AM now One with The Perfect Life of Complete Wholeness.

Mind and Spirit do not become tired nor weary, and I AM Mind and Spirit.

I AM free from all illusions of weariness.

I AM alive with the Great Vitality of the Spirit.

I AM receptive to Truth and can understand it.

I AM one with a complete understanding of Truth.

I AM free from every belief in pain.

Spirit cannot feel pain, and I AM Pure Spirit.

I AM happy and complete, today and forever.

I AM Peaceful; I AM calm I AM secure.

I AM now in complete harmony with the Whole and I cannot lose nor misplace anything.

I AM constantly finding more and more Good.

I AM complete within myself; I AM perfect within myself; I AM happy and satisfied within myself.

I AM immune to all suggestion and cannot receive false thoughts, nor harbor them.

I AM surrounded with a circle of Love and Protection.

Asleep or awake, I AM free from false thoughts.

I AM Spirit and cannot take on the fears of the world.

Every thought that I think, I think in oneness with divine wisdom.

Every word that I speak, I speak in oneness with divine truth.

I live and move and have my being in the infinite sea of divine spirit.

The future is mine. I have the power to determine what it shall be.

I have faith in God, I have faith in man, I have faith in myself.

I rejoice eternally that I AM blessed with the precious gift of existence.

I AM filled with the fullness of health and shall always be perfectly well.

I AM living the one life and that life is infinite, perfect, divine. With God all things are possible, and I AM eternally one with God.

I live and move and have my being in the infinite sea of omnipresent good.

I AM filled and surrounded with infinite power, infinite
wisdom, infinite love.

I have found the true life, and I have learned how to live.

I AM able to do whatsoever I will to do, for I AM spirit, and
spirit is above limitations.

I AM loving, tender and sympathetic; just, truthful and
sincere; patient, gentle and kind.

Whatsoever I will is good, for my will is divine will, and divine
will is infinite will.

Whatsoever belongs to God belongs to me, for I AM a child of
the Supreme and heir to His Kingdom.

Whatsoever is in God is in me, for I AM created in His image
and likeness.

All good is in the spirit, and the spirit is in me; therefore all
good is in me.

I now realize the perfect health that is in me, and in that
health I shall ever live.

The real substance of my being is always wholesome, always
clean, always in health, strength and harmony. I AM That.

I AM perfectly well through and through, for I AM made of
that substance that is always in perfect health.

I AM living forever in the kingdom of good. Therefore I shall
always have abundance of everything that is good. Limitless
supply is mine.

I AM a spiritual being. The spirit is the everlasting home of joy. Therefore my ways are ways of pleasantness and all my paths are peace.

I AM free from all disease, all misfortune, all sorrow, all want, all ignorance, all evil. I AM living in the truth and am perfectly free.

I forgive everybody to the utmost for what they might have done against me, and ask everybody to forgive me for what I might have done against them.

All the souls of the universe are my brothers and sisters; we are all children of the one God; we are all rays of the one Great Light; and in this spiritual unity I shall ever live.

Peace is mine, freedom is mine, health is mine, power is mine, strength is mine, abundance is mine, wisdom is mine, joy is mine, love is mine all good things are mine.

I think the good, speak the good, act the good. I seek the good and find only the good. I attract the good and radiate the good. I AM surrounded by the good and live the good. Nothing but the good can proceed from me or come to me.

I AM now and by this act of mind recognizing my own identity with the One Creative Mind.

I AM a center in this One Mind Universal which operates wholly by affirmative thought.

I AM aware that my constructive thought for myself and others is Creative Mind producing. My thought is reinforced by the Power of the Whole.

I AM now emerged through the veil of limited and "personality" thinking. I AM thinking with all the authority and power of the One Creative Principle.

I AM the self-renewing Life of the One Mind. I AM now expressing all the vigor and beauty of Eternal Youth and Creative Power in all my thought and action.

I AM a great stream of radiant Life, Light, Love and Strength to all my world. This radiance dissolves and brushes away all sense of doubt, fear and inferiority both for myself and for others.

I AM seeing and knowing that I AM even now a center for loving and original service to others. I AM giving so richly and intelligently that riches come streaming back to me.

I AM the Mighty Power of Mind, concentrated in me to create forms of beauty and harmony in this one spot where I AM a focal point for service.

I AM the Mighty Power of Creative Thought seeing all things perfect. I think, believe, and act as though my desires for Prosperity, Health, Productiveness and Happiness were inevitably to be answered.

If I AM conscious of being free, secure, healthy, and happy, I sustain these states of consciousness without effort or labor on my part.

Man cannot possess more in the visible world than he is conscious of in the invisible world or realm of Mind.

Keep these words in mind. Repeat them over and over to yourself while going about your day, and you will find that your breathing will accommodate itself to the thought you have in mind.

IF YOU WILL CONTINUE, day after day, to meditate upon the above fundamental truths, WITH SINCERITY OF HEART AND AN OPEN MIND, your BELIEF IN THEM will become a part of your very being, and you will find the EFFICIENCY AND POWER OF YOUR LIFE IMMEASURABLY INCREASED; you will become a veritable DYNAMO OF CREATIVE ENERGY, and your work will become easy and pleasant.

SO LONG AS YOU THINK IN TERMS OF LIMITATION, you will be limited, but just the moment you come to realize the God-like powers within you, holding the Divine Image in which you were made, firmly in mind, you will know the TRUTH and the TRUTH will set you FREE . . free from doubt and free from disease, free from poverty, free from unhappiness, and by this power you will CREATE YOUR LIFE STRONG AND BEAUTIFUL.

I leave you with a few words from Joseph Murphy. . .

**As you go to sleep tonight, practice the many techniques**
which we occasionally refer to. Repeat the word, "Wealth,"
quietly, easily, and feelingly. Do this over and over again as a
lullaby. Lull yourself to sleep with the one word, "Wealth."
You should be amazed at the results. Wealth should flow to
you in avalanches of abundance; this is another example of
The Miracles of The Subconscious Mind.

# Quote Resources

The quotes, meditations and affirmations in The Power of I AM, Volume 2, are from the following authors.

Fay Adams, U. S. Andersen, Raymond Charles Barker, M. MacDonald-Bayne, Joseph Benner, Kate Atkinson Boehme, Thomas Parker Boyd, Louise Brownell, H. Emilie Cady, Robert Collier, Florence Gloria Crawford, Mrs. Dan M. Davidson, Walter Devoe, Franklin Fillmore Farrington, Charles Fillmore, Emmet Fox, John Seaman Garns, Harry Gaze, Neville Goddard, Henry Hand, Shirley Bell Hastings, Ernest Holmes, C. W. Kyle, Christian D. Larson, Elinor S. Moody, Joseph Murphy, Janeski Robenoff, Robert A. Russell, John Milton Scott, Elizabeth Towne, Thomas Troward, Helen Wilmans

Thank you for purchasing The Power of I AM - Volume 2

## BOOKS BY DAVID ALLEN

The following books, either edited and or compiled by David Allen, in paperback and (some in) hardcover, are available on Amazon as follows...

**"The Neville Goddard Collection" (All 10 Books Plus the 1948 Class Lessons and the July 1951 Radio Talks)**

**The Power of I AM**

**The Power of I AM - Volume 2**

**The Power and The Law of Faith**

**The Definitive Christian D. Larson Collection (6 Volumes - 30 Original Larson books in all)**

**Neville Goddard**
**Your Inner Conversations are Creating Your World**

Also check our growing selection of books on Kindle.

Thank you!

**I AM Notes and Personal Affirmations**

CPSIA information can be obtained
at www.ICGtesting.com
Printed in the USA
BVOW08s0720111117

500065BV00002B/54/P